Conversations With God:

An Ordinary Life in the Hands of
an Extraordinary God

By Sondra Leigh Haggard

CONVERSATIONS WITH GOD- An Ordinary Life in the Hands of an Extraordinary God.

Copyright © 2023 All rights reserved— Sondra Leigh Haggard

Please direct all copyright inquiries to:
B.O.Y. Enterprises, Inc.
c/o Author Copyrights
P.O. Box 262
Lowell, NC 28098

Paperback ISBN: 978-1-955605-34-2

Cover and Interior Design: B.O.Y. Enterprises, Inc.

Printed in the United States.

Dedication

Dedicated to Daniel and Arnelle Helbling

Acknowledgements

God is the Alpha and the Omega. Since He is the Alpha, I want to acknowledge Him first and foremost. How grateful I am that He is a hands-on God who loves me more than I can comprehend! He has chosen to speak to me throughout my lifetime and has given me the grace to recognize His voice. Without Him, there would be no book to write.

Daniel Helbling, to whom the book is dedicated, is the one who truly held me accountable to start writing. His excitement about the book, before a single word had been written, helped me garner the courage to begin. The twinkle in his eye when we spoke encouraged me and his faith in me strengthened me when I felt far too inadequate for the task ahead. Daniel joined the Lord in eternity before the manuscript was complete, but it is quite possible that I would still be waiting to write the first word if it were not for his encouragement and excitement. Arnelle, his wife, shares the dedication. She was my first editor and has been equally excited and encouraging. She is a dear friend who loves the Lord with a deeper understanding of what it means to fully love and trust God than anyone else I know.

I have learned so much from my pastor, Jerry Keller. Pastor Jerry unapologetically preaches the message of the Kingdom of God, seeking it first, and being obedient to the voice of God when He speaks. This message has revolutionized my life. I know with all that is within me that my eternity will be significantly better because of the years I have spent under his ministry. How great is the debt of honor that I owe to Pastor Jerry! Additionally, this acknowledgement would become a book unto itself if I were to try to fully describe the wonderful Godly attributes of his wife, Susan, and the friend, supporter, and prayer warrior she has been in my life.

Each of my children, Ben, Diona, and Alanna, as well as my son-in-law Will in more recent years, have been used of God to speak into my life. This is also very true of my sister Leanne, who is one of my greatest supporters and someone I can always trust to both seek and speak truth.

When a time came that it was difficult for Arnelle to continue assisting me as editor, Ron Hyink stepped into the gap and assisted me greatly. He was also very enthusiastic about this project, and I appreciate his wife, Becky, allowing him so many hours of time to edit the initial manuscript.

Elizabeth Doss introduced me to my publisher, Otescia Johnson. God orchestrated the meeting to be sure, but without the obedience of these two women to His prompting, this book would likely still be a manuscript.

Wayne, you are my rock and a quiet pillar of

strength. As I try to put into inadequate words what you mean to me, I find my eyes welling with tears. I may be able to put a sentence together, but I find I am failing when it comes to fully expressing what you mean to me. Thank you for the hours you allowed me to write, always supportive and encouraging, and never begrudging a single minute that I spent at the keyboard. You have been a type of Christ in my life—redeeming, healing, and loving me from almost the first moment we met.

As God is not only the Alpha, but also the Omega, I want to also acknowledge Him at the end. He knows the end from the beginning. He desired this book to be written before I was born. His ways are perfect, and His love is immeasurable. Thank you, Father.

Table of Contents

A Note from the Author

When I sat down to write this book, it was of the upmost importance to me to share everything God wanted me to share. I have peace knowing I have accomplished that goal. To properly share everything, it was paramount that I change the names of some of the people who are involved to protect their privacy and identity. All other details in the book you are about to read are true accounts of experiences and conversations I've had with God. I pray my conversations are the launching pad for your own intimate encounters with our Heavenly Father.

Foreword

Mark Batterson has become one of my favorite contemporary writers. He conveys ageless Biblical truths in fresh and relevant ways. I heard him say recently that he primarily writes for future generations. That is a concept that gripped me because speakers and writers are always challenged to know your audience, know to whom you speak. Bill Johnson, another accomplished author, is a fifth-generation pastor on his father's side and fourth on his mother's. He states in the introduction of When Heaven Invades Earth that "I only wish I had another chance to hear their stories and to ask them the questions I never had asked as a young man. It would mean so much more to me now."

Sondra has written in such a way that future generations will be able to hear those things that would otherwise be lost. The review of key moments in her life not only has the potential of teaching us but can impact those yet to come. There needs to be more, not less, effort made to record our journey. You hold in your hand an effort that will not only teach valuable lessons but should inspire you to record your own.

Review is a lesser-known spiritual discipline. The

Bible commands us to engage in that way and yet we seldom do. A model is set before us in the Bible itself. Furthermore, Malachi tells us of a "book of remembrance" that is being written even now. It is for future generations. The residents of Heaven will be reading the unknown stories of spiritual pilgrims. It will be good reading.

As a pastor, I am very thankful when people learn to "connect the dots." Sondra has done excellently in that way. You will be able to see images appear from the efforts of her remembrance. The stories required both courage and vulnerability to share. May we each be inspired to tell our story in such a way that God is glorified, and followers are encouraged.

A fellow pilgrim,

Jerry D. Keller
Pastor, Plainfield Christ Fellowship

Preface

Why write this book? The primary reason from my point of view is obedience. Quite simply, after having four people from different parts of my life over the course of four weeks tell me "You should write a book," I asked God if He was trying to tell me something. He responded by giving me the title. His purposes? I can only speculate unless He reveals them to me at some point in the future. Perhaps there is something in me He wants to change or develop; perhaps there is something in you. He may simply want me to record these conversations for myself to review and increase my own measure of faith. Possibly, it is as simple and yet as profound as to awaken in you a hunger to talk with God, to believe that if someone as common as me can converse with the Almighty, then so can someone like you. For I believe with all my heart that if I can hear the voice of God, you can also.

For clarity, I have not heard the audible voice of God. There are those who claim to have heard His voice, and I believe it can and does happen. How wonderful, magnificent, humbling and terrifying that must be! But so far that is not how God has chosen to speak with me. I am open to that when and if He chooses.

My conversations with Him have been no less clear for having not been audible. Yet, at the risk of sounding contradictory, sometimes I have had to seek Him for understanding. In the end, this is a book of reminiscences. I hope you enjoy reading about the journey He has taken me on, but more importantly, I truly hope it opens your eyes to the many ways God speaks to His children and ignites in you a desire for a more intimate relationship with our Father.

Chapter 1

Secret Sisters

As a young mother, I was employed full-time outside the home and full-time inside the home. I had strayed from the faith of my youth, perhaps having never fully embraced nor understood it, and had recently returned to God, attending church at the same church my parents attended. I was in the first few years of my second marriage. I was, like all young mothers whether employed outside the home or not, tired. It was February and, in Indiana, that means it was cold. I had just returned home to my husband, two small children, and a toddler after a long day in the pharmacy, having been on my feet all day.

The phone rang and it was my mother. "Do you want to go to the Secret Sister banquet tonight? We're taking the church bus; and if you want to go, I'll have them wait for you."

"No," I responded. "I'm too tired to go. I'd have to get cleaned up and change clothes. I can't."

"Are you sure?" she pressed gently. "Yes, I'm exhausted," I replied.

"Well, call me if you change your mind."

"I will, but I won't change my mind." With that, we ended the call.

The Secret Sister banquet was an event where the Secret Sisters of the previous year were revealed, and new names were drawn. Secret Sisters left small gifts, notes, and cards for each other throughout the year, especially on significant days—holidays, anniversaries, birthdays— but the primary responsibility was to pray for your Secret Sister regularly. The challenge was to find a way to get through the year without revealing who your Secret Sister was until the next banquet. This would have been my first opportunity to be and to have a Secret Sister.

As I walked away from the phone intending to rest, I heard in my mind as a thought, "You're going to the Secret Sister banquet."

"No, I'm not," I replied to myself.

"You're going to the Secret Sister banquet," my mind repeated.

"No, I'm not!" I emphasized.

"You're going to the Secret Sister banquet, and you're going to draw Hattie Richwald." My mind was awfully specific this time.

"Now I know I'm not going!" My knee-jerk reaction was both adamant and rebellious.

Hattie was a sweet woman of about the same age as my parents, but at one time she revealed to me that she was the mother of a woman whose close childhood friend was my husband's former wife. Because of the suspicion I held towards my husband's former wife, anyone who had a relationship with her was inherently untrustworthy in my mind. And, in what horrible way did she mention this? At a surprise baptism for my husband on the same day my two older children were baptized, she leaned forward from the pew behind me to whisper it in my ear. She said she was so happy for my husband and had been praying for a decade that he would find God, love, and happiness in life.

In my moment of extreme happiness, finding out about this relationship had burst my bubble. I immediately determined to stay away from Hattie and her daughter,

Annette, even though they were part of my church family. They were now suspect, and I had no trust in them. Up to that point in time, I had been successful in my avoidance.

"You're going to the Secret Sister banquet, and you're going to draw Hattie Richwald!" This time the voice in my mind was quite firm. Suddenly, I realized that I was arguing, not with myself, but with God. Hearing from God like this—a conversation—had never happened to me before! I hurried to the telephone and called my mother. I gave her a brief synopsis of what had just happened and asked her to have them hold the bus for me. I had only a few minutes to get cleaned up and changed, but I did so in record time. As the last one to arrive, I climbed aboard the bus and tried to mentally prepare for what lay ahead.

At this point, it would be nice to say that the bus ride was uneventful. However, that was not the case. I don't remember from all those years ago whether this occurred on the ride to or from the banquet, but it was dark, and enroute the bus's headlights quit working. While the bus was not quite filled to capacity, the women who were riding on it prayed for God to repair the headlights, which came back on and worked for the remainder of the trip.

The banquet itself was light-hearted and fun. I sat next to my mother, and we chatted with the women around us throughout the meal. After the meal, we filled out Secret Sister forms about ourselves—favorite color, collections, birthday, anniversary, personal trivia. These forms were placed in a paper sack. There were about 50 women represented altogether. Most had ridden on the bus, a number had driven individually, and quite a few had sent completed forms with someone else because they couldn't make it to the banquet but wanted in on the Secret Sister fun.

I was about the fifth person to draw a name. I reached into the bag, drew a breath and a form. Sure enough, I drew out Hattie's form. My heart sank. By this time, my mom had also drawn a form. I tilted my form so she could take a look at it, and I sighed. She showed me hers. She had drawn Grace Bartlett. Grace is a beautiful, sweet saint. I would have loved to have drawn Grace's form. Mom loved both of these ladies. She whispered, "I'll trade you."

"Are you kidding!?! No way!" I responded. I might not have been happy about the circumstance, but after having already argued with God, there was no way I was going to add an act of total rebellion now that He had proven Himself to me in this way. The banquet over, we put our forms into our respective purses and headed home. I was now officially Hattie's Secret Sister.

I determined in my heart that I would be faithful to my commitment to pray for this woman I wanted to avoid. And, I determined that she would not lack the little surprises and cards on special days, even though I had no desire to have a relationship with her. Within a few months, I learned a truth that I have since seen play out many times over. If you faithfully pray for someone, God will change your heart towards that person. Within a few months, I began to feel a desire to spend time with Hattie, and not long after that, I began to love her.

In a short time, she and Annette became two of my dearest friends in the Kingdom of God. Our children played together. We spent time together in laughter, in tears, in counsel, and in prayer. While our children are now grown, we moved apart geographically and Hattie has since entered into eternity, to this day I love these two women deeply. The memories of our years together and the hugs we shared still bring a smile to my face and joy to my heart.

A year later, on another cold, dark February night, it was again time for the Secret Sister banquet. I loved Hattie deeply and was looking forward to revealing to her that I had been her Secret Sister that past year. I had a beautiful gift for her for the reveal—a rain stick that I knew would bring her joy. I pulled into the parking lot at the site of that year's banquet and, in the dark, a woman walked in front of my parked minivan. "That's who you're going to draw this year," God whispered. This time, I recognized His voice immediately, so I knew better than to argue. The woman, Eleanor Tichenor, was not someone I knew except by sight. I really knew nothing of her personally, and my only impression was from having overheard someone say something negative about her to someone else. What injury our casual words can have! We never know who might overhear and what pain our unguarded, unsanctified speech may cause. As it turns out, God had work for me to accomplish in the future, and this wrong impression about a beautiful woman who was His child needed to be changed.

By the end of the banquet, I had revealed myself to Hattie. It turned out God had revealed to her the work He was doing in me, so she already knew that I had been her Secret Sister. It was no less sweet. And, I had drawn Eleanor's form. While I still had some desire to draw someone I already loved, I recognized the work God had done over the past year and looked forward to seeing what was next. I again determined to be faithful to the commitment I had just made, without her knowledge, to Eleanor.

Over that year, God again worked the same love miracle in my heart toward her as He had with Hattie. We did not become the close friends that Hattie and I had become, but I loved Eleanor and saw in her a kindness and sweetness that I did not previously recognize. I also found that she had an intense love for her husband and children.

Eleanor lost her battle to cancer shortly after that. In subsequent years, God was able to use this story of His love for Eleanor through me to minister to her young daughters who have since grown into strong, faithful women.

While I continued as a Secret Sister for several more years, the women whose names I drew after that were always a surprise. Funny thing—I don't remember whose name I drew the next several years or even if I ever drew Grace Bartlett, but I will never forget the two years and the two women through which God worked out His plan for me. I am so thankful He taught me to recognize His voice.

Chapter 2

Neon Sign

While my children were young, I worked as a hospital pharmacist on the overnight shift. The schedule was Monday through Sunday, working a 10-hour shift each night from 9 p.m. until 7 a.m. Then I would have the following week off. Having every other week off was quite an enticement, and this rotation is something I have worked for a total of seven years of my career to date. Over the years, it has allowed me to spend a lot of time with my children that working a day or evening shift would not have.

At this hospital, I was allowed two 15-minute breaks, which I could combine for one 30-minute break as long as I took it during a prescribed hour and carried a pager. The pager was important, as I was the only pharmacist in the hospital during those hours and the pharmacy had to be locked down if I wasn't inside. Typically, I would lock up the pharmacy and go to the cafeteria with my technicians and attempt to have a meal. If I was paged, I and one or both of my technicians would return to the pharmacy to take care of the need. Uneaten food would go into the trash.

Looking back, I wonder why I continued to try to have a meal each night, as on any given week, I might get to eat one or, at most, two of the meals I purchased. On the night in question, my technicians and I had just sat down at the table and had not yet even begun to eat when the pager alerted me to call the Emergency Room. I rushed to the phone at the other side of the cafeteria and called in.

"We have someone going bad and the doctor wants Cardizem IV STAT!" the voice on the other end of the phone said when I identified myself. I acknowledged that I understood and let her know the drug would be there right away. When I hung up, I motioned to my technicians to continue eating, as I felt no need to interrupt their meal for this easy request. They would take care of my tray if I didn't return. My plan that night, however, was to grab the drug and send it by our tube system to the ER and then return to eat my meal. After all, while I was typically interrupted on my break, it was rare to be interrupted more than once, and I anticipated this request wouldn't take more than five minutes. I ran up the stairs, as that was the quicker route to the pharmacy from the cafeteria than taking the elevator. I keyed in the code to the pharmacy and ran to the first most likely place for the drug to be located.

It wasn't there.

I ran to the second most likely place.

It wasn't there.

I ran to the pharmacy storeroom, where we had large rolling shelving units stocked alphabetically with drugs.

It wasn't there.

I knew we had this medication in stock. It was a new drug at the time and, while I had not yet actually seen it, one of our clinical pharmacists had written an informational flyer about it, and I had read the flyer earlier that night. I was feeling panicked, as I was acutely aware that my inability to locate this drug was using up precious minutes that could result in loss of life. Maybe, I thought, this one had been alphabetized by generic name. I moved down to where the drugs starting with a "D" were located.

It wasn't there.

My panic increased. I looked up and cried, "God, where is it!?!" Immediately, before my eyes appeared a scrolling neon sign. "LOOK IN THE FRIDGE." That started my feet moving again. I ran to one of our five refrigerators. It was the correct refrigerator. It was double-sided. I opened the door to the correct side. There were three shelves and three drawers on this side of the refrigerator. I opened the correct drawer and put my hand immediately upon the vial! I ran to the tube system, packed the vial so that it would not break during the trip to the emergency room and sent it. I then sank into a chair, meal forgotten.

I later heard the patient lived.

I have reflected on this conversation with God many times. There are so many questions I still consider from time to time. Why use a scrolling neon sign to communicate with me? Why didn't I just marvel in amazement at what I was seeing, wasting precious time? How did God then direct my steps to the very refrigerator, door, drawer, and place where the drug was stored? Did the patient ever sense the miracle God worked through me that night to preserve his life?

I don't know the answers to any of these questions, but I know God wanted a specific life preserved. I know He didn't want me to live with regrets for not delivering the medication in time. I know He is a God of infinite variety who speaks in the moment in the method that is best for the situation at hand. And, I know He hears me when I cry out to Him.

By the way, I've often thought the sign said "FRIDGE" because there wasn't time for me to read "REFRIGERATOR."

Chapter 3

Uneasy Feeling

I was working an overnight shift at a different and much larger hospital. Here, I supervised four technicians on the first three nights of my rotation and three technicians for the last four nights. We delivered medications on the hour to one side of the hospital and on the half hour to the other side. We also took care of STAT orders, filled outpatient prescriptions for patients seen in the emergency room but not admitted to the hospital, filled medication carts with the next day's medications for the inpatients, and changed the nutritive water for the medicinal leeches whenever we had them in stock. All of us worked pretty much non-stop from the moment we arrived until we left for home the next morning. There was never time to waste in this busy hospital.

An order came to the pharmacy for gentamicin, which is given intravenously. Gentamicin is an antibiotic that must be carefully dosed based upon each individual's kidney function. Both the dose and the dosing interval are important. The dose must be high enough that the peak level will be effective against the bacteria, but not so high as to damage the patient's hearing. The interval between doses has to be long enough to allow the level of the gentamicin to drop below a certain threshold to allow the kidneys some relief so as not to damage them. So, there are numerous calculations done over the course of therapy that require a number of blood draws from the patient.

One of my technicians entered the order, and I needed to check it before it would be mixed in the sterile IV room. It is imperative to not introduce any contaminants into a patient's veins, so there are special rooms, sterile environments, and scrubbing and gowning procedures in hospital pharmacies similar to what happens for surgeries in order to ensure the product remains uncontaminated as it is prepared. I checked the order, and it was entered exactly as written, but I felt uneasy about it. I looked at it again. There was nothing inherently wrong with the order. The dose and dosing interval seemed appropriate. It was entered for the patient on the order. It had been requested in an appropriate amount of fluid. Everything looked fine, but my uneasiness grew.

I called the nursing station, not even knowing what question to ask. I no longer remember exactly how I phrased it; but basically, I asked the nurse if she was sure the order was correct. She was sure. My technician, confused about why I was delaying this order, asked if she could mix it now. I started to tell her to go ahead, but I couldn't shake the uneasiness. I told her to wait while I called the nurse again.

This time, I knew even less about the question I should ask. However, I was honest with the nurse and told her I had no idea why, but I felt uneasy about the order. I requested that she review it one more time to be certain it was correct. She responded testily, expressing the need for this IV medication to be delivered right away. I did not feel better about the order when I hung up the phone. At this point, the technicians had begun to talk among themselves, one generous speculation being that I was overly tired. Being tired was certainly a common occurrence for those of us who work long overnight hours. All of my technicians could appreciate that possibility. Again, I was asked if the medication could be prepared.

"Just wait a minute," I responded.

"For what?!" she retorted, less than generously.

I didn't know. I just couldn't shake the uneasy feeling I had about this order. I checked a few other orders and then convinced myself that I was indeed simply overly tired, ignoring the fact that I wasn't having the same uneasy feeling about any of the other orders I had just checked.

"Go ahead and mix it," I conceded. As my technician walked toward the sink to scrub before preparing the IV, the pharmacy phone rang. It was a different nurse from the same unit. She had been on break, and when she returned, the nurse I had spoken to previously had complained to her about the pharmacist—me. She looked at the order she had transcribed and immediately realized she had entered it for the wrong patient. She would be sending a corrected order down shortly.

I hung up the phone and told the technician to prepare the dose, but to wait for a changed label. I don't know if I was ever able to adequately explain what had happened to my technicians. I don't know what they ultimately thought about the whole encounter. But, I do know they no longer thought I was just overly tired. And, I know I learned to hear God's voice in a new way.

Chapter 4

The Question

"I brought you here to get your question answered," God whispered to my heart during the sermon that Wednesday night. It got my attention! What unanswered question did I have that God wanted to be certain was answered?

Wayne and I had been married by the wonderful pastor of a church we had been attending in Martinsville, Hoosier Harvest. We loved our pastor. We loved our church. We were living in Shelby County, so it was a long drive for us, although the teaching and the worship were worth the drive. Even if we had not felt that way about the teaching and worship, God had clearly placed me in that body before Wayne and I met. So, we made the hour long drive each way every Sunday.

About a year into our marriage, we began to feel that the distance was causing us to miss out on fellowship with the body during other church functions and felt a desire to be more connected. As we discussed options—moving, driving more—we came to the consensus that

God was calling us to be part of a different body. We both believe that God places each of us in specific church bodies and that we are to fully commit to where He has placed us, moving only when He directs. We weren't certain how to find the place God had for us next other than to begin visiting churches.

We had visited two or three churches when I happened to drive by Christ Fellowship of Indianapolis on a lunch break from work. Years before, I had attended a revival at my previous church home for which a pastor from a Christ Church Fellowship on the East Coast had been the guest speaker. I had been very blessed during that week and had thought in my heart that, if God ever moved me from my home church, I would very much like to find a Christ Church Fellowship to attend. It turns out there are none in our area, but the name of this church was close enough to catch my attention. The next day, I deliberately took my lunch break to stop by this church and ask about service times and dress codes. I was able to speak with the associate pastor who was friendly and welcoming. I told Wayne about the church, and we agreed to visit it on Sunday.

We were warmly greeted and could feel the presence of the Holy Spirit during the worship, and the sermon was on the Kingdom of God. We felt it was possible we had found God's place for us. The following Sunday we returned, and our children Ben and Alanna accompanied us. The sermon was on another aspect of the Kingdom of God. We all felt confirmation that we were now placed in the body of Christ Fellowship of Indianapolis, and so we committed to attend.

The following Sunday we were invited to a pitch-in lunch at the church. Rotating groups of church members met for fellowship each Sunday. We attended and were able to spend some time speaking with the pastor, Jerry, and his teenage son, Taylor, who, years later, would become our associate pastor. Having heard three sermons now where the topic of the Kingdom of God was a major part and having never really been taught about it, I asked the pastor, "What is the Kingdom of God?" He told me that he had a book I could borrow and asked Taylor to go to his office to get it. Taylor returned with Pastor Jerry's personal copy of The Unshakable Kingdom and the Unchanging Person by E. Stanley Jones.

Years later, Taylor told me that the book, now out of print, was important to his father and that he had never seen him loan it to someone on a first meeting. It was not long after that first meeting when I recognized the Holy Spirit had knit our families' hearts together that day. Pastor Jerry allowed me to keep the book for several months. It is an exceptional book, but unlike most books for me, not one I could read quickly.

After only a few months, we asked to be accepted as members of the church and soon found ourselves attending Sundays and Wednesday nights and becoming part of the choir. Even though we had come from a more charismatic background than this church seemed to be, we were learning more about the Holy Spirit and the importance of obedience than ever before. We were hungrier for this than we had been aware, and every opportunity to learn more found us at the church. The Wednesday night when God told me He had brought us here to get my question answered was only about six months into our attendance.

"What question?" I silently asked when nothing came to mind. I waited, listening both to the sermon and for God to help me know what He was trying to tell me. In a few minutes, a discussion from about eight years earlier came to mind. At that time, I was a member of the church my parents were attending when the pastor spoke on Peter's confession of Jesus as the Messiah found in Matthew 16:13-20. In verse 19, Jesus states, "I will give you the keys of the kingdom of heaven …." During the sermon, that phrase caught my attention, and I wondered what the keys of the kingdom of heaven are. It was not the focus of the sermon; in fact, other than being read as part of the scripture passage, it was not discussed at all. I made an appointment to meet with the pastor. We talked for about 45 minutes that day and in answer to my question, "What are the keys of the kingdom of heaven?" I had received the answer: "It's a mystery that no one really understands." While it felt a bit unsatisfying, I knew there is much we will not know or understand on this side of heaven, and so I accepted the keys of the kingdom as one of those things I would learn about in eternity.

I had forgotten my question of some eight years prior, but God had not! Wayne and I have been a part of Pastor Jerry's ministry for nearly 21 years now, and we have learned much about the keys of the kingdom of heaven, and we continue to be hungry to learn more! The Kingdom of God is as vast and eternal as its King, Jesus Christ!

Chapter 5

Healing is Available

I was deeply wounded. My second marriage was in the process of being dissolved and the pain was incredible. Regardless of the reasons for divorce, it is always a tearing apart of a relationship that was intended by God and by the married couple, to have been permanent. Even when, in some measure, the dissolution of the covenant is a relief, it still creates deep wounds, some within the marriage itself and always more at its end.

Prior to the actual beginning of legal proceedings, the deterioration of my marriage had thrown me into a deep despair that I thought could only be relieved by ending my life. After an attempt that was thankfully not actually planned out, and as such, had virtually no chance of success, I found myself sitting on the floor of my doctor's office. He had the wisdom to send me to the hospital for a short psychiatric stay.

During that week, I wanted only my children to visit and my Bible. My sister Leanne brought both. When I wasn't speaking with the doctor or therapist or getting involved in a group session, I pored over my Bible, looking for comfort. I almost exclusively read Psalms. One night as I was reading and crying out my fears, pain, and desperation to God, I suddenly found myself sitting in His lap! This was the most intense manifestation of God as my Father I have ever experienced. I was keenly aware that I was His child, that He loved me, and that He was holding me in His lap as an earthly father holds his child who is hurting. From that moment, I knew I could continue. I was still wounded, still hurting, and still grieving. There was still much to endure, but I knew in a fresh and personal way the love of my Heavenly Father, and that gave me a significant measure of hope and strength.

Discharged from the hospital, I knew I needed to find a place to worship. The church I had attended for the past 10 years was the background for the majority of my marriage, and there were individuals there who had contributed to the wounds I received. As it turns out, it would be many years before I could visit that church without reliving the painful aspects of those years. I am thankful that, through forgiveness and healing, I can now remember the vast amount of good that I experienced in that decade and the things I learned of God without rejecting all of it because of the painful end. I began visiting churches with my children. Ben suggested we go to a church in Martinsville called Hoosier Harvest Church. I knew nothing of this church, but knew of no reason not to visit it, so we decided to attend there the following Sunday.

We were welcomed warmly and, as worship began, found the worship style was similar to what we were accustomed to experiencing. In the middle of a song, God whispered to me, "There is healing available for you here." I continued to worship through tears. The pastor was young and energetic. His preaching style was engaging and enthusiastic. I have no memory of the sermon topic, but in the middle of the sermon, God again spoke to me, "There is healing available for you here." I knew I needed healing desperately. The search for a church home ended.

This was a growing church and, in an effort to remain personal and connected, there was a small group program. I was assigned to one of the small groups. These met on Wednesday nights and a program for children was available at the church on the same night so that parents could attend their small group. In addition to the small group, I met with Pastor Chris from time to time for counsel and prayer. While I was receiving healing, I was also receiving fresh wounds as my divorce proceeded.

One day, as I was receiving counsel over the phone from Pastor Chris, he stated he knew something that could help me and asked if he could call me back. In a few minutes, he called back to say there was a women's retreat that weekend in Brown County and there was one opening. If I could commit right then, I could have that spot. I committed. Two days later, I drove to a beautiful setting in Brown County to attend a retreat with Tree of Life Ministries. I have tried to find out occasionally during recent years if this ministry is still active but have not found them online. I hope they are, because they worked tirelessly and compassionately with God to bring emotional healing to wounded individuals.

I won't disclose everything that happened during this retreat as I want to respect their program; however, at one point, they instructed each of us to find a spot inside or outside where we could comfortably be alone with God and to begin reading in Isaiah 54, continue through chapter 55, and stop at the verse where God stopped us. Then, we were to ask God why He stopped us at that verse.

I found a peaceful setting outside under a tree and sat down with my Bible, paper, and pen. I began reading, but began sobbing as I read verse four, which in the NKJV states, *"Do not fear, for you will not be ashamed; Neither be disgraced, for you will not be put to shame; For you will forget the shame of your youth, And will not remember the reproach of your widowhood anymore."* It didn't take a lot of insight to realize I had been stopped.

When I had composed myself, I asked God what He was trying to say to me. God began speaking to me immediately. Revelation came as fast as I could write and faster than I could comprehend. I was transcribing a flow of information and words of love, vision, and healing more quickly than I could absorb. In the end, I received about six handwritten pages from God. Hidden in the middle was a single sentence that I didn't notice at all. In fact, when I read to the group what God had given me, I still didn't notice that sentence. It would take weeks and several additional readings before that sentence registered at all. And when it finally did, it was not a welcomed word. That, however, will be a topic for another chapter.

That long weekend and the information I received from God about myself in relation to Him was the beginning place of true healing. There remained a long road ahead, but seeds of healing were sown in a place that would receive the right amount of care. There would be much time before the harvest was ready, but at least it now lay ahead.

Chapter 6
Timely Visitor

Geriatric pharmacy is my passion. I am blessed to be working as a Long-Term Care pharmacist, so the vast majority of my patients are elderly. For the first four and a half years with this pharmacy, I served as a consultant pharmacist, going out to nursing homes and reviewing charts to help the rest of the healthcare team optimize care through appropriate drug therapy. This gave me a little leeway with regard to my schedule.

This particular morning, I was headed to Lawrenceburg to conduct chart reviews at a facility there. I had been up for a fair bit, had showered and dressed. I was updating my computer with the latest drug files for the facility from the pharmacy and would then head out the door. As I put my laptop into its case, I had a strong impression that I should stay home. I hesitated for a moment, but it was a workday and I continued toward the door to the garage.

The impression to stay at home grew stronger. Like everyone, I've had days where I'd rather stay home than go to work, but this was something different. I loved my job, and I was fully ready to go to work. Wayne was already at work, so I couldn't discuss this strange impression with him. Finally, I decided that I would go to Lawrenceburg the next morning. I had planned an office day at home for tomorrow, so I would simply use today as my office day instead.

I got my laptop back out of the case and began working on the reports I needed to complete. I also kept a few chores running in the background—laundry and dishwasher. I was thus occupied when the doorbell rang. I certainly wasn't expecting anyone, especially since no one would have expected to find me at home on a weekday. I went to the door and found a man I didn't know standing there. I opened the door a few inches.

"I'm in the neighborhood taking care of some trees for your neighbors, and I wondered if you wanted this tree cut down," he stated. "Since I'm already here, I can give you a better price than if you would want it done another time. I'm bonded." I looked at the paperwork he offered then out at the tree he was indicating. It was a very tall oak tree with a diameter of somewhere around two feet. I liked that tree. It was majestic and, standing only about 15 feet from the front door, the shade from its leaves and branches helped to keep the house cool in the summer. It had withstood the winds from the tornado that had recently passed close by unlike some of the trees in our neighbor's yard. Why, I thought, would I want him to cut down that tree?

"What would you charge?" I heard myself ask to my own surprise. He named a price. I had no frame of reference for determining whether the price was fair. I asked him to wait while I called my husband. I called Wayne at work, something I tried to avoid. There was no phone in his department, so I had to call the office, and someone would have to go get Wayne and bring him back to the office to take the call. I told Wayne why I was home, what was going on and the price the man had quoted. Wayne felt it was a fair price and that the tree should come down. So, I gave permission for the oak tree to be cut down and went back to my reports and chores. Sometime later, the doorbell rang again. The tree was down, I paid the man and went back to work.

In those days, Wayne would typically arrive home mid to late afternoon. When he arrived home, he had me come outside to look at the tree stump and the remains of the trunk that were still in the yard. The inside of the trunk was largely rotted away. It is amazing that the oak tree had not fallen on the house during the recent severe weather. And, there is no doubt that had we not had it safely cut down, it was destined to fall in a storm to come. How great is our God!

Chapter 7

God Speaks Through Ben

My children were taught from an early age that God wants to communicate with them, that while reading the Bible is a primary method through which He speaks to us, it is by no means the only method. Because of this, one of the ways God has been able to speak to me is through my children.

I was asked to lead a praise and worship team at the church I was attending. I had been a member of another team, and that worship leader felt that God had told him it was time to move on to other areas of ministry. After prayerful consideration, I felt that God wanted me to step into that role. When I met with the pastor to accept, he told me to take my time building the team and explained that there was no hurry for the team to have a name, but that once it was named, it was permanent.

Over the next several weeks as the team came together, I was spending time considering names for the team. I had several desires for the direction of the team. I wanted the praise and worship to be a conduit for bringing people into God's presence. I wanted the team experience to be uplifting and Spirit-filled. I wanted our praise to bring pleasure to God. In considering these desires, I began to consider the thought of our praise being a sweet aroma to God. So, I began to search scripture for the verses talking about the sacrifice of praise and of sacrifices being a sweet aroma. My hope was to then use my Strong's Concordance to find a Hebrew or Greek word or phrase that meant sweet aroma.

After some weeks of research, I felt I had the team's name determined and planned to tell my pastor the following Sunday. The next afternoon, my teenage son, Ben, said to me, "Mom, God doesn't want the name you decided on. He is going to name the team." This was a moment of choice for me. I had put a lot of time, consideration, and effort into the name I had chosen. I felt it made a statement about what I thought the team was to become. Did I believe God could speak to my children? More than that, did I believe God could speak through my children to me? I chose to be humble in that moment, thinking I was choosing humility for the sake of my son and his walk with God.

That very night, I had a dream. In this dream, I was sitting in the front row of a university-style auditorium. I was directly in front of the lectern. The auditorium was dark except for the lectern area and a circle of light in front of it which included my seat. No one else was seated in the room. I could not see who was at the lectern, but I could see his hand gesturing toward me. The gesture was an added emphasis of direction to the words that were being spoken. "You will name the worship team Expectation. You will expect My presence in practice and in worship. You will expect My imminent return."

When I awakened, I had no doubt that God had spoken to my son the day before. Likewise, I had no doubt that God had named the worship team. I communicated the name to my pastor who asked if I was sure, since there was no going back. I was sure. God had spoken.

I soon learned that we also had a genre assignment that aligned with the name. We were to use only songs that were about presence, intimacy, and relationship. Every time I tried to introduce a song to the team that lay outside of our assignment, we simply couldn't learn it. Even if it was a song that each of us knew individually, we were unable to put it together as a group. It didn't take long for me to stop trying to step outside of the assignment!

Over the time that Expectation existed under my leadership, we did have the pleasure of practicing and worshipping in the Lord's presence. The practices and times of leading others into praise and worship of our King remain some of the most precious times of my life.

Though those days are more than two decades behind me now, I still enter into praise and worship expecting the presence of the Lord. I also still expect His imminent return.

Chapter 8
Cloud Elevator

When you are a mother of three children, one of the most treasured times of each day is the moment they are all successfully in bed for the night. Granted, you never know whether they are down for the entire night or if some need will arise in the middle of it that will require Mommy or Daddy. This particular night, I was truly down for the count. I can't recall now what had occurred that led to this state of exhaustion, but the children had been in bed long enough that I was also in bed and soundly asleep. Typically, when one of my children came to me in the night, I became alert quickly and took care of the need, whether it was scooting over so the child could climb in to be comforted following a nightmare or getting up to attend to sickness. This night was different.

Alanna, who was then 5 or 6 years old, came into the bedroom. I'm not certain how long she shook my shoulder or how many times she said, "Mommy," but I know she had to put some effort into waking me up. I opened my eyes to see a very sweet, but also very frightened, face.

"Mommy, there's something bad in my bedroom," she said. I wasn't really awake enough for that to fully register. She must have realized that, so she repeated it urgently.

My sleep-deprived brain was craving sleep more than it should have upon hearing that statement from my young daughter. I rolled over to look straight in her fearful eyes and said, "You know Jesus loves you and you love Jesus, right?"

"Yes, Mommy," she replied.

"You know that nothing bad can stay where Jesus is, right?"

"Yes, Mommy."

"Go back downstairs to your bedroom and tell the bad thing it has to leave in Jesus' name. Just say, 'In Jesus' name, go away and don't come back!' It will have to leave."

"Okay, Mommy," she said with complete trust in me and in Jesus. She left the bedroom and I instantly fell back to sleep. Sondra Leigh Haggard

In the morning, I woke up in a panic. Had I really, truly sent my baby downstairs to tell a demon to leave her bedroom? Had I not gone with her? Had I simply fallen back to sleep? I was definitely not feeling proud of my parenting skills. I threw on a robe and rushed to Alanna's bedroom. She was sleeping peacefully, but awakened as I knelt by the side of her bed.

"Mommy!" she exclaimed; her eyes filled with wonder. "Jesus rides a cloud elevator!" This was not at all what I expected to hear. Relief washed over me instantly.

"Tell me about it," I replied.

She then described how she had come downstairs to her room and commanded the bad thing to go away in Jesus' name just as I had instructed. She said it left, so she climbed into bed to go to sleep. When she had lain down, she saw Jesus come down from the sky on a cloud elevator. She described Him as wearing a very shiny white robe and she couldn't see His face because it was as bright as the sun. When He got to her level, He said to her, "I'm proud of you for obeying your Mommy. Because you did, your family will be protected." When He had said this, He rode back up into the sky on the cloud elevator.

In my sleep-deprived state, I had spoken truth to my daughter, truth that I believed and taught her to believe. But even today, it is hard to comprehend that I didn't get out of bed and go downstairs with this tender child. So much more amazing, however, is that Jesus loves me and my children so much that He covered this parenting mistake in such a way that it was fully and completely redeemed beyond my wildest expectations. He showed Himself strong to Alanna and me. At the same time, He also demonstrated His great power and love.

Chapter 9

A Prayer for Protection

Dinner was over and the children were preparing for bed. By this time, they were mostly self-sufficient in this area with only Alanna needing direction. I was blessed with children who were fairly compliant with bedtime, so when pre-teen Ben came out of his room, I didn't immediately think he was working his latest bedtime delay tactic.

"Mom, I have a really bad feeling about my window," he said, concerned.

"What do you mean?" I asked.

"I don't know, it just doesn't feel safe," was his response. His father and I walked to his room. The window didn't appear compromised in any manner. Nothing could be seen outside that was not always outside. Of course, it was now fairly dark, but even turning on the outside lights revealed only what was always in this peaceful Brown County setting—a large yard, beautiful trees, our garden and the sides of the pond that could be seen from Ben's bedroom window. The weather was clear, no storm was impending, and the breeze was calm.

"Everything looks fine, Ben," one of us said.

"It still doesn't feel right to me," Ben responded.

"Let's pray about it," I suggested, having no other idea how to handle Ben's fear.

Ben thought that was a good idea, so I led a prayer for protection and safety for anything that would try to come through that window. This appeased Ben and he went to bed. Somewhat later, we also went to sleep for the night which passed uneventfully.

The following morning, as I was preparing breakfast, Ben burst out of his room. "Mom," he exclaimed. "You've got to see this! Come here!" I hurried to his room.

"Look!" was all he said. I looked around the room for what had him so stirred up. My eyes went across the window and immediately back to it. I ran out of Ben's room, yelled for my husband and, without waiting, went out on the wraparound deck. A large tree had fallen during the night directly away from Ben's bedroom window! All five of us had slept peacefully through what must have been a mighty crack and crash. The tree was large enough that Diona and Alanna used it for a balance beam for some time afterwards.

What might have happened if Ben had ignored the warning the Holy Spirit was giving him? Or, if having received and relayed the warning, what if I had simply told him everything was fine and sent him to bed? While I do not know with absolute certainty, I believe the tree would have fallen on the house and come through that window. Whether or not there would have been injuries, we would certainly have had damage to our home.

Sometimes, when I think about this, I reflect that God could have simply chosen to keep the tree from falling. He could have let it fall but directed its path away from our house without any forewarning. He is God, after all. Instead, He chose, as He so often does, to involve His children in His plans. This helps us to grow in faith, obedience, and trust in Him and in His voice. It teaches us to still ourselves to listen, and to have a relationship with Him in the moment, knowing that He loves us completely.

I still marvel that He speaks to me. It never grows old or mundane.

Chapter 10
Do You Love Me?

I was sitting at the dining room table, working on a Bible study that our church provided. Each individual study was dedicated to a single book of the Bible or a part of a book with the exception of the introductory study. I was working my way through the Gospel of John, Chapter 21, and as I completed the three verses in which Jesus asks Peter three times if Peter loves Him, I heard God whisper to me, "Sondra, do you love

Me?"

"Yes, Lord, I love You," I responded immediately.

I began to reflect on what this question might mean, but very quickly, I heard again, "Sondra, do you love Me?" "Yes, I love You," I said.

This time the question came even more quickly.

"Sondra, do you love Me more than your job, more than your home, more than your husband, more than your children?"

I began crying. "No, Lord, I don't love You more than these, but I want to."

That moment of honesty before God opened the door to a journey of deeper love for Him. It is not so much that intense love for God filled my heart and everything else paled in comparison. Instead, it revealed my current reality—that I loved my companion, my children, and my life more fully than I loved my Savior and Creator. It also opened my eyes to the fact that I had a desire to love God more. That one moment of intense honesty changed my perspective. From that moment on, I began to grow more in love with God. And, I have found that loving God more, putting Him first, only increases my love for my husband, my children, my family and other people as well. God's economy is so different from ours, especially when it comes to love.

I began to pray and seek to love God. I began to try to put Him first, failing in one instance and succeeding in another. And as the years passed, I would reflect and realize that I did indeed love Him more. A few years after the Columbine tragedy, I remember reflecting whether I loved Jesus enough yet that I would not deny Him if faced with death. As I considered this question, I realized that I always would have protected my children in any circumstance and would have easily chosen my death over theirs. My love for my children is fierce. I also realized that would not have always been true of my love for Jesus. Yet on this day, as I reflected on those tragic events and the condition of my own heart, I understood for the first time that the thought of denying my Lord grieved me deeply. In that moment of self-reflection, I came to the realization I finally loved Jesus more than life. While that is as yet untested and I don't seek or desire that particular test, I still believe it to be true.

Many years later, in November 2012, I was in Israel, and we stopped at the Primacy of Peter, which is the spot along the Sea of Galilee where the event of John Chapter 21 occurred. As I walked on the rocky beach area, God reminded me of our conversation some 15 years earlier. In that moment, I realized that if He were to ask me if I loved Him more than my husband and my children, I would again have to answer, "No." I still wanted to, and the truth was that my love for Him had grown so much deeper, but I had not yet fully given Him first place in my heart.

I believe now that I may have grown complacent at some point thinking that I had arrived. God desires and deserves so much more than complacency. He desires intimacy and deserves my first and best efforts, not my leftovers. Here, on a rocky beach where Jesus walked with Peter and the other disciples, He walked with me and helped me make a fresh commitment of love to Him.

This change has been a journey, rather than an

instant transformation. Today I can say that, given the choice between my husband and my God, I will choose God. Given the choice between my children, my parents, even my life and God, I will choose God. There have been times I have made those choices. Each time, God has proven Himself faithful. Even when it seemed that choosing God over a loved one in a situation risked damaging the relationship, I have found that choosing obedience to God is the better path. To date, I have not lost a relationship because of faithfulness to Him. After all, my husband, my children and my parents do not belong to me. All that I have belongs first to God and I am only the caretaker.

And my life? I cannot even draw my next breath unless He wills it. My life, my family and my relationships are safe in His hands. The question is never whether God will be faithful to what I have committed to Him, but whether I will be a faithful caretaker of what He has committed to me. Still, if the day comes when I choose God and lose a relationship, it remains true that I would not profit in retaining the relationship if I lost my soul.

I continue to pray that God will help me to love Him more. I believe that my heart—human, finite and scarred by life—is not capable of loving God in the infinite manner of which He is worthy. So, I continue to ask God, Who is love, to change my heart and to make it capable of loving Him the way He deserves to be loved, and He continues to answer. My heart is still finite, and many scars remain, but by His grace, I love Him more today than yesterday and so much more than the 20 or so years ago that we first had this conversation. By His grace, tomorrow I will love Him more than I do today.

Chapter 11

Dancing with Jesus

In the mid-1990s, I had an opportunity to attend the first week of a two-week conference in South Carolina hosted by Rick Joyner's Morningstar Ministries. I had heard about it through my pastor who was organizing a group of people to go to the second week of the conference. At the time, my work schedule was seven days on, seven days off, and I was scheduled to work the second week of the conference. I was initially disappointed that I would not be able to attend, but then realized there was no reason I could not attend the first week of the conference. My husband agreed that I should go, and so I made arrangements with the conference and booked flights to and from South Carolina.

I am an extrovert by nature, but I was nonetheless a bit intimidated to be alone in the sea of people I found at the conference. If memory serves me well, there were in excess of a thousand people for the first week of the conference, and I was there unaccompanied. It did not take long, however, to find myself immersed in the teaching and worship. I interacted with others at the conference during meals and breaks, but mostly found myself wide-eyed, taking in this new experience. Never before had I been so immersed in such a sea of fellow believers.

As the week continued, I found myself to be a sponge, soaking up incredible teaching, hearing prophetic words, both corporate and personal, and worshipping. There were many gifted and anointed speakers—Jack Deere, Bob Jones, Mike Bickle and Rick Joyner were there—and the worship was beyond anything I had so far experienced. Imagine a thousand voices united in worshipping Jesus! There is power in the worship of a single individual. How much more power exists in the worship of a thousand people in unity!

As is the case in any gathering of this size, there were many different types of people with different backgrounds, beliefs, and worship styles. It would have been easy to become distracted by the differences, but I took to heart a word of direction from Rick Joyner on the first day. He said that we were free and encouraged to worship as the Holy Spirit led us to worship. However, he realized that it was likely that we could observe some who we would feel were worshipping in the flesh. He instructed us to not allow that to distract us or prevent us from entering fully into what God had for us.

Rick then told of a time when he had observed

someone worshipping in the flesh rather than in the Spirit. When he began to judge that difference in his heart, God spoke to him and admonished that He would rather the person worship Him in the flesh than other things he could be doing. And so, when I was tempted to distraction by the multitude of different worship styles around me, I would close my eyes and focus on worshipping the King.

This has since become my personal habit. Whenever I am worshipping God in a group setting, I close my eyes so I can focus on Jesus. After all, if I am focused on whether or not someone next to me is raising their hands or expressing some other form of worship, I am not truly worshipping. I become, at best, an observer and, at worst, a judge.

Toward the end of the week as we were going from a time of exhortation to a time of worship, Rick felt a very specific song should be a part of the worship. The song he had in mind, however, was still in the process of being written by David Ruis, a songwriter and the very one who was leading worship at that time. David nevertheless chose to be obedient to the leading of the Holy Spirit and led us in worship with his new song entitled, "We Will Dance."

As we learned the song, the thousand voices surrounding me became more confident and stronger and the worship intensified. And, as the words became familiar, I closed my eyes and sang to and of Jesus. "And we will dance on the streets that are golden, the glorious bride and the great Son of Man…." Suddenly, I was unaware of the crowd surrounding me. The music became a peaceful backdrop to an incredibly intimate moment. I was dancing with Jesus! Everything that was reality in the world at that moment fell away as I swayed in the arms of my Lord. I cannot tell how long we danced. It was over too quickly and yet was satisfyingly long. As far as we count time, the dancing ended before the song did, but as God exists outside of time, it was an entire dance for me. I wanted to remain in His arms forever.

This dance with Jesus remains one of the sweetest moments of my spiritual life. When I later became the leader of a worship team, it was my goal to create an atmosphere that would enable others to experience similar moments with God. The enemy wants to steal such moments away from us. In fact, dance is an area in which I later experienced a severe emotional wound. I stopped dancing. God has let me know He wants me to dance for Him again. The enemy wants to keep me from dancing by convincing me that opening myself up to dancing will inevitably lead to being wounded again.

So far, God has healed me of this wound to the point that I want to dance for Him again. I know His perfect love casts out all fear, so I look forward to the day when fear is cast off and I freely dance before my Lord. But, this spiritual dance with Jesus is something the enemy has not been able to steal away. It is mine forever and it remains with me as a sweet foretaste of dances to come, an eternity of dances with Jesus.

Chapter 12

Angel at the Wheel

Winter in Indiana almost always brings ice. This particular winter day I was working until 9 p.m. in Franklin, about a 25-minute drive from our home out in the country. While I worked the decidedly slow shift, rain was falling steadily outside and arriving in the form of ice. By the time I closed the pharmacy, there was a very thick layer of ice covering everything, about three-quarters of an inch thick. No wonder business had been so very slow! I walked very carefully to my car and wondered if it even made sense for me to try to drive home in these conditions. At that time, there were not really many options for overnight accommodations in Franklin, and sleeping in my minivan wasn't wise or appealing. I decided I would drive home.

It took about 30 minutes of effort to get the van door open and to scrape a hole through the ice on the windshield that I could see through. I only managed to get about a six-inch-diameter hole scraped. Fingers numb and tired from both the workday and the ice removal efforts,

I climbed into the van and started it. I thought that I would allow it to warm up and see if that would melt additional ice from the windows. After 10 minutes or so had passed, I realized that the heater from the van was struggling to make a difference. And so, I decided it was time to begin the trip home.

As I began to put the van into gear, fear began to overwhelm me. Driving on ice on straight, treated roadways is dangerous enough, but I was about to drive on untreated roads with a number of turns, intersections and, once I reached the country, hills and curves to navigate. Making matters worse, I had very limited visibility through the windshield and no visibility through the side or rear windows. A tap on the brakes at any time could put me in a spin, a ditch or worse. I was well aware that my minivan was not known for stability on icy roads. I left the van in park and began to ask God for safety this night.

After a few minutes of prayer, I put my foot on the brake and put the van into reverse. Fear threatened to paralyze me. I began to sing a worship song that spoke of God's protection and provision. Fear backed off a bit, and I slowly lifted my foot off the brake. I carefully backed the van out of the parking spot and changed gears. Fear seemed to be my undesired companion for this trip, but I continued singing which kept fear's power over me Conversations with God limited. I moved slowly through the parking lot and to the light which would allow me to enter the road for the long trip home.

I began to wonder how I would stop should the light turn red at any of the intersections I would be driving through. Then, I began to wonder how the cross traffic would stop if I had a green light. I continued singing. Fear backed off again. When I got to the first light, it was green. I didn't need to brake and there was no cross traffic! I slowly turned onto the road and my journey began. "Jehovah Jireh, my provider, His grace is sufficient for me, for me, for me," I sang, continuing to use songs of provision and protection to keep the ever-present fear at bay. As I came to intersection after intersection, I would see headlights and taillights of cross traffic, but when I would arrive at the intersection, the light would be green and no cross traffic would be there. Still, I had no need to brake.

"Oh, Lord, my Rock, my strength in weakness, come rescue me, O Lord," I sang. I remember emphasizing the part about being rescued! Fear continued to be restrained by worship and I continued driving. In one particularly scary moment, I felt the rear end of the van begin to fishtail. Even before reflexes could kick in to counteract the movement and long before I consciously thought of what correction would be safe, the fishtail corrected itself. I changed to songs of thanksgiving and considered that it almost felt as though something had picked up the rear end of the van and straightened its course.

"Give thanks with a grateful heart, give thanks to the Holy One," I sang as I safely turned onto the country road that would begin the last few miles to the house. Now I had hills and curves to navigate, but I was unlikely to have any other traffic to worry about at this hour and in these conditions. The last few miles passed without further incident. Finally, I arrived home safely, exhausted and with a bit of a sore throat, after nearly 90 minutes. I stepped through the garage door into the family room and collapsed onto my knees from a combination of weakness and a desire to thank the One who had gotten me home safely.

Alanna, who was probably 7 or 8 at the time, came running down the stairs to where I knelt. She threw herself into my arms and, breathless with exertion and excitement, cried directly into my ear, "Mommy, an angel flew the van home!"

"Yes, Honey, he did," I replied, knowing in that moment that it was true.

Chapter 13
Learning to Trust God

"I am preparing a man for you." It was one sentence buried deeply in the midst of six pages of things God had spoken to me about myself and His plans for me. I had read those six pages a number of times without that sentence making its way into my consciousness. I read it again to be sure it was really there, and I had not misread it. Surely it actually said something like, "I will be your husband" or "I will be your covering" or, better yet, "You will have no need for a man in your life." But, no, clearly written in my own handwriting was, "I am preparing a man for you."

Divorced once, I had still believed in marital happiness and had remarried, but now I was going through my second divorce. I no longer believed that I should be married. I no longer desired to be married. I had no intention of ever marrying again. In fact, the idea was abhorrent and frightening in equal measure.

"I am preparing a man for you." Once this declaration made its way into my awareness, I first tried to ignore its existence. For some weeks, I tried to pretend it wasn't there, that I had not heard it, written it, or read it, but this proved impossible as it would play over and over again in my mind. Next, I tried giving this unknown man away. "Give him to someone else," I prayed. "I've had two husbands and there are women who've never had one. Give him to one of them." God's response was silence.

"I don't want another husband," I prayed on another occasion. "I really don't need one."

Silence.

This continued for weeks. Over and over, I would explain to God why preparing a man for me was not smart. I would reject this man I had yet to meet. I would plead for God to change this plan. After all, we hadn't met yet as far as I knew, so it couldn't possibly be too late for a revision. Surely there was a Plan B for me that did not require a husband.

Silence.

Week after week, as I pled with God to change His mind and His plan, He responded with silence. Finally, about three months after the Tree of Life ministry retreat, I was praying in the car as I was driving. This time, I defiantly thought I had the matter figured out. I knew what God hadn't considered when He decided to prepare a man for me. "Okay, God," I challenged. "You're preparing a man for me." It was not a true concession. "Tell me then," I continued, "How will I ever trust a man again?" Surely God would see the impossibility of this happening and would relent of this totally undesirable plan.

After weeks of silence, God spoke to me again. "First," He whispered, "you have to learn to trust Me."

"I do trust You, God!" I cried out.

The silence returned. I had to pull off to the side of the road as I began crying. In the newly returned silence, I was convicted of how I did not trust God at all. Sure, I trusted Jesus' incredible sacrifice for my salvation, but that wasn't enough. I did not trust the heart of the Father. He was saying to me, "I have a gift for you," and I was responding with "I don't want it." I was not trusting that He truly loves me. I was not trusting that He only wants what is best for me and that He knows what that best is. I thought that I knew more and that I knew better than God. That desire for self-arrangement with its mindset of superiority is the very opposite of trust.

Broken and sobbing, I sat by the side of the road and, when I could speak again, began confessing my lack of trust to God. "You're right," I agreed with Him. "I don't trust You. Teach me to trust You."

How I have come to love the conviction of the

Holy Spirit that leads to repentance! I have found that when the Holy Spirit points out something that is wrong in me, it means that He is ready to help me change. If I agree with Him in that moment, change will occur. Sometimes the change is instantaneous; sometimes it is a process. Either way, I have found He knows the right time to put His finger on the wrong thought process or sinful habit for true change to occur. He knows when I am ready to hear, and He knows when He is ready to do the work. My agreement with Him in the moment was both an invitation for Him to proceed and acknowledgment of my desire to be who He designed me to be.

I have often heard people talk about how much this hurts, typically followed by a comment to the effect that the suffering is worth the end result. My own experience has been vastly different. The only time this is truly painful is when I fight God, trying to hang on to my pride. The pain is in the self-arrangement, in the time between His revelation of the issue and my acknowledgment of His sovereignty, the interval during which my carnal flesh is trying to retain control and be lord of my life. When I agree with God immediately, humbling myself before the One who knows me better than I know myself, there may be brokenness, but there is always relief.

In that moment of confession and agreement, I was cleansed from the sin of not trusting the only One who is worthy of all trust and my heart began to change. I began to truly trust God. This particular change has been one that was both instantaneous and a journey. Yes, I immediately began to trust Him; but trusting God is something that is required daily as I choose whether or not to believe Him when He speaks, as I choose whether or not to obey Him in the moment, and as I choose whether or not to become discouraged when His promises seem to be delayed. I have found Him to be completely trustworthy and, where I am still waiting for Him to provide what He has promised, I choose to trust, knowing that when the provision arrives, it will be perfectly timed.

Wayne and I have been married 21 years as of October 6, 2022. He has been a type of Christ in my life, loving me unconditionally and used of God to bring significant healing to my heart. I'm so thankful God brought me to a place where I could trust Him enough to accept the man He had prepared for me.

Chapter 14
Go Slow

Alanna had been homeschooled her entire life, but with the changes in circumstances that divorce had brought into our lives, it became necessary to enroll her in school outside of the home. I didn't feel clear with the idea of moving her directly from the intimate and controlled homeschool setting into the sixth grade at a large public school, so I began researching area private schools. Eventually we settled upon a small Lutheran middle school intending to transition her to public schools when she entered high school. Her transition to public school actually came seven years later when she attended Purdue University.

As with most private schools, the school transportation system consisted of parents' vehicles. The school had perfected a drop-off and pick-up procedure that kept traffic flowing at the start and finish of schooldays and ensured student safety. After messing that up at the first pick up, I quickly learned the procedure and adjusted my work schedule to accommodate twice daily visits to the school which was about 10 minutes from the job I had at the time as a home infusion pharmacist. To discourage student tardiness (really this was to discourage parent tardiness), the school had a policy that if the student was dropped off more than five minutes late, instead of simply letting the student out at the door, the parent had to go into the office and sign the student in for the day. The stated reason for this policy was student safety, and while I can see the logic behind that, for me it was more about discouraging tardiness.

Typically, I enjoyed the drives to school and back home with Alanna. The drives gave us some one-on-one time that blessed both of us. This particular morning, however, everything was going to have to go right in order for me to be able to drop Alanna off at the door. Normally I dropped her off a bit early so I could be at work by 8 a.m., but things had not gone smoothly at home that morning. So, I was focused on whether red lights were going to turn green (or green to yellow) and how much I could push the speed limit and remain both safe and ticket-free. While the trip had not been without conversation, I had not carried my end very well.

Almost there and still edging toward the five-minute limit, we were stopped at an intersection waiting for a left turn arrow. I was watching for the cross traffic signal to turn yellow so that I would not waste even a second when the left turn arrow turned green for me. Pulse fast and poised to accelerate, I focused on the traffic signal. I saw the light turn yellow for the cross traffic lanes and my pulse increased, and I began to move my foot from the brake when I heard, "Go slow." Recognizing the voice of the Holy Spirit, I increased the pressure on the brake pedal and waited as the left turn arrow changed to green. The cross traffic had stopped, their light now red and I eased into the intersection. Including the left turn lane from the opposing direction, I had four lanes to cross. As I came even with the second lane, a car ran the red light in the last lane! I estimate that the car was going in the neighborhood of 50 mph. Had I continued with my original plan, we would have been broadsided by that vehicle and Alanna would have taken the brunt of the impact.

Shaken. but very thankful, we safely and more cautiously completed the remainder of the drive to school. On the way, I told Alanna why I had slowed down, and we praised God together. Then I very happily got out of my car and signed her in for the day in the office. I no longer had any concern about arriving late to work either.

I've always known that Alanna would have been severely injured had that accident occurred and that I would most likely have been injured as well. Many years after the fact, I was recounting this story and the Holy Spirit whispered to me that Alanna would have been killed and that I would have been severely injured. How horribly different life would have been, I actually can't imagine or contemplate. But God, who is merciful and loving beyond my comprehension, chose to warn me and preserve us that morning. I am thankful He taught me to recognize and respond to His voice.

Chapter 15

Forgiveness

Jesus taught His disciples to pray that they would be forgiven as they forgave others. As His disciple, this also applies to me. This has been an incredibly difficult teaching for me. Am I not forgiven if I harbor unforgiveness toward others? Can my lack of forgiveness exclude me from spending eternity with God? I don't claim to know the answers to these questions. Sometimes it seems so clear and other times so incredibly muddy. What I do know is the miracle of forgiveness I experienced, and the true change forgiveness makes when it happens.

Like most people, I have received my share of mistreatment at the hands of others. Some of it has been through no fault of my own and some of it happened as a result of my own poor choices. I have had plenty of opportunities to forgive. I have learned, for most things in life, there is no need for forgiveness when I choose simply not to be offended. This is radically different from the current mindset I see around me where it seems that many people spend their days looking for ways to be offended. I try to consider what I know about the person I'm interacting with and to interpret what was said or done through that lens. When that doesn't clarify the statement or action sufficiently, I go to the person and ask gently for clarification. Typically, everything is immediately cleared up with no opportunity for offense or wounds and the resulting bitterness to take root. That leaves the bigger issues.

Over the last several decades, I have read a number of good books on forgiveness. I have walked through the recommended steps. I have prayed, asking God to help me to forgive. I have asked for prayer that I would be able to forgive. I have spoken aloud that I choose to forgive and then asked God to turn my choice into reality. I have prayed for the welfare of those who have hurt me. I have worked hard at the act of forgiveness. To be fair, I have had a measure of success, but true heartfelt forgiveness had eluded me.

I've also tried the whitewashing route. I tried to convince myself that when the Bible states to live peaceably with others insofar as it is within my power, it only referred to other believers. That took a few people off my need-to- forgive list. Yet, I've realized, who am I to judge? I've tried to convince myself that as long as I didn't actively wish harm on another individual that I had forgiven that person. For some people, getting to the place of not actually wishing they would experience harm was a big step, but this was still short of true heartfelt forgiveness.

Periodically, I would either read a Bible passage regarding forgiveness or would hear a sermon on the issue, and I would again take this to God. Sometimes I would gain ground; sometimes not so much. I became accustomed to carrying this weight to the point that I mostly didn't even perceive that it was still there.

One Sunday morning, I walked into church to find myself literally face to face with someone who was a part of my past. Actually, I knew to expect that person to visit that Sunday, as my pastor had mentioned him the week prior. What I didn't expect was coming around a corner and nearly bumping into him, nor did I expect the extreme emotional reaction I would experience. This person had caused serious harm to a number of people whom I cared about deeply, including members of my own family. I had not spent the week anticipating his visit, so I was surprised at the magnitude of the reaction I was feeling—fear, anger and pain welled up in me to such a degree that I had to leave the building. I walked outside, praying, until I had myself under control and felt I could go back inside.

As I re-entered the building, service was beginning. I thought I had my emotions in check until I realized that this person would be taking an active part in the service. I ended up spending the entire worship time praying that I would be able to get through the service, that I would be able to pay attention to the sermon, and that I would be able to remain in my seat until the service was complete. While I disciplined myself to take notes during the sermon, I also cried out to God to prevent this person from causing any additional harm to anyone in our church.

Throughout the service, I was fully aware of a call to truly forgive this person. I was perhaps even more aware of the fear that the idea of forgiveness carried with it. If I forgave him, didn't that give him greater ability to cause harm in the future? If I forgave him, did that mean I was required to fellowship with him again? I found myself in a tremendous battle. I did not want to be disobedient, but I also did not want to forgive this man.

After service, I went outside with my associate pastor to discuss the dilemma I found myself in. We both committed to pray about it and to reconnect later in the week. Through circumstances outside his control, my associate pastor and I didn't reconnect until the following Sunday; however, God had no circumstances beyond His control, and He and I did connect. As I prayed that week, I had gotten to the point, not of forgiving, but of wanting to forgive. When I reached that point, God stopped me and clearly told me, "That's enough for now." So I set the issue aside except to let my associate pastor know that God had worked a change in me.

Some months later, my pastor again mentioned

that this same individual would be back in church the following week. Having no desire for a repeat experience of such overwhelming emotions, I started talking with God about it right away. I was asking God a number of questions. I wanted to know what forgiveness meant with regard to trust, fellowship and fear. Did true forgiveness mean I would need to pursue a relationship with the one I forgave? Did forgiveness require extending trust to the one who had previously proven untrustworthy? How much future pain was I opening myself up to if I forgave, trusted and pursued renewed relationships?

Because of these unanswered questions, I was truly afraid to forgive this person who was associated with one of my deepest wounds. Still, on Thursday morning of that week on my drive to work, I prayed and told God I was ready to forgive. As I was walking from my car into the building where I work, a semi was headed in my direction. The turn signal was on, signifying that the truck would be turning many yards before my intended path across the lane. Nonetheless, I waited to begin crossing until the truck actually began making the signaled turn. The Holy Spirit spoke to me in that moment about the relationship between forgiveness and trust. "Forgiveness can be like that," He said. "You can wait until you see the person begin to make the change before you trust again." In that moment, the fear that I was required to extend trust as a part of forgiveness lifted off me. It was another step forward.

That Saturday morning, I knelt to pray before starting my day. I have become aware that I have an assignment to pray for a number of pastors, their families and their ministries. This started with an assignment to pray for my pastor and his family and over the years has grown to include many other pastors, families and ministries, one of which I haven't even met yet and a couple that I've only met once or twice. I try to start each day with prayer for them and for my own family and any other commitments to prayer I have made for that day.

This day, God had a different agenda. As I began to lift up the first pastor, God spoke to me that today was the day for forgiveness. I began to cry, not out of fear or dread, but out of a hope and trust that something new was about to happen. God began to bring face after face to my mind's eye, the first of which was the man who, with his family, would be in church the following morning. "Yes," I cried as each face appeared before me. "Yes, I forgive." Faces I had forgotten appeared. Faces representing small offenses and large—each face I saw I agreed with God that I forgave. Some were more difficult than others—the man who had raped me when I was 16 and my girlfriends who had assisted him in it, my ex-husbands, a former pastor—and some were easier to forgive. "Yes, yes!" I cried after each face, hesitating a moment here and there at some of the most difficult to verify within myself the truth of that cry.

Finally, the faces stopped coming. I thought that forgiveness was complete, and I felt both spent and elated. Yet as I continued to kneel, marveling in the work God had done in me, He gently admonished me to forgive Him next. This shook me for a minute, as He is perfect and therefore can have done nothing wrong, nothing needing forgiveness. Yet I realized there were things I had questioned, things I really thought should have been, could have been, different. And so, I forgave God. Once I accepted the need to do so, that forgiveness was actually quite easy and something of a relief after the weightier choices. I moved some of the weight off my knees, preparing to stand. "Wait," He said. "Now you need to forgive yourself."

Forgive myself? I began sobbing anew. I was willing, but even after so much forgiveness had been extended and experienced, I felt unable to forgive myself. I had made so many wrong choices over my life. I had caused myself so much pain and had put myself in situations that allowed others to hurt me deeply. Who deserved blame and unforgiveness more than I? Still, God had walked me through so much in the last hour, couldn't He also walk with me through this? Wasn't He telling me He was ready to do so? Wasn't He telling me I was ready to do so?

"I forgive …," I started and then stopped, sobbing too hard to continue. Did I really deserve forgiveness? In a few moments I tried again, and again could not continue. Finally, on the fifth attempt, I was able to say, "I forgive me!" It was truly done. God had worked a miracle of forgiveness in my life! I had only to cooperate.

When I stood up from my place of prayer, I felt completely elated. I had a sense of being truly forgiven of my own sins, completely washed clean, as though it were the first time that was fully true. I saw a glimpse of myself in a gleaming white robe and realized a transformation had taken place. I also felt physically lighter and realized that, while I had not lost any weight in the physical realm, spiritually, great and heavy chains of bondage to each person I had forgiven had fallen off me. I was spiritually lighter and I felt it in a very real and physical sense.

None of the people I forgave, including myself, deserved forgiveness. Forgiveness is not about what is or isn't deserved. It isn't about whether there is repentance offered or restitution made. It's about obedience to God who sent His Son to pay the price for all sin. Jesus didn't require apologies, and certainly no restitution was possible as He hung on the cross and said, "Father, forgive them."

Since that day, I have learned the truth that withholding forgiveness doesn't punish the ones who offend. It punishes the one who is holding onto the offense. In me, there been enough wounds and sufficient lack of forgiveness that a certain amount of bitterness had taken root in my life. The complete forgiveness that God walked me through uprooted the bitterness and removed it as well.

Sunday brought proof of Saturday's victory! I entered into worship fully. I concentrated on what God was saying through the sermon. I enjoyed the time with my church family. And, I was able to have a pleasant conversation with the person who had wounded so many that I care about. In fact, I apologized for not having done my part to make him feel welcome on his previous visit. For several years, I prayed for him and his family as I prayed for the others God has assigned to me. I did so, not only out of obedience to the God who loves me and has delivered me, but also out of a true desire to see their lives blessed.

I plan to be vigilant to ensure that I am never again enslaved by a lack of forgiveness. I want to be completely confident when I pray that the Father forgives me that I have also forgiven others.

Chapter 16

Servant of the Month

The pastor at the church I was attending gave out a "Servant of the Month" award, alternating between male and female servants each month. He would ask God who should be honored, and the pastor alone knew who would receive the award each month. He announced it the first Sunday of each month by giving a description of the areas in which the person served, then gave the name of the individual at the end. As the congregation applauded, the new Servant of the Month would then walk to the pulpit, shake hands with the pastor and receive a nice ink pen on which was inscribed a phrase of appreciation and the name of the church.

I can't say how this program of appreciation affected others, but I would sit in anticipation as the description was being given, trying to determine who was being described, and every other month wondering if it would be me. To be fair, I didn't always wonder if it would be me, but as I became more and more active in various church ministries, I would grow excited as the time came for the award to be announced and then deflated when, month after month, I was not the one being described.

I continued to serve when asked, never turning down an opportunity to volunteer or a direct request for involvement. I truly enjoyed being a part of the ministries of the church, but as months went by without recognition, I began to feel unappreciated. I did feel that everyone who was chosen as Servant of the Month was deserving, but wasn't I deserving as well?

One day, I took my discouragement to God. I reminded God of the many ministries in which I was involved and, stressed that more weeks than not, I was in the church building every day of the week. Why didn't He tell the pastor that I should be the Servant of the Month? God was ready for my petulant question. "You will be Servant of the Month when you no longer feel the need to be," was His reply.

I was taken aback by that response, and at first I didn't even understand the issue. My basic personality type is such that I not only am unafraid of the limelight, but I tend to crave it. I needed praise and recognition. I needed to shine and perform. I desired the accolades and appreciation of others. This was the foundation I had built my structure of self-worth upon. Surely the God who created me understood that. Why wouldn't He grant that need?

Eventually I realized that understanding was only going to come from the same source that had answered my question. I began asking God to help me to understand what He meant and what change needed to occur in me. First He led me to Jesus' words in Matthew Chapter 6, "Be careful not to practice your righteousness in front of people, to be seen by them. Otherwise, you will have no reward from your Father in heaven."

To be fair, a lot of ministries are in front of people and this was true of most of the ministries I was involved in. There was no way to continue my ministry involvement and not be seen by people. However, as I considered Jesus' words, I began to realize that I had allowed a desire for recognition to create a slight change in my motivation for ministering. I wanted "to be seen." It wasn't the reason I had entered into a ministry, but I had allowed it to become a part of ministering after the fact.

This, I think, is one of the most difficult areas of spiritual growth to deal with—removing what is not good from what is. The vast majority of the ministries I was involved in were what I was supposed to be involved in. I'll discuss that more fully later. All the ministries I was involved in I had agreed to be a part of because of a desire to serve God. That was good. Yet because of my personality, I had allowed an unholy desire for recognition to creep in. As I recognized this, I agreed with God that I had developed some wrong motivation and began to ask

God to remove this desire from me and to purify my motives. This began a journey of taking wrong thoughts captive, repeated repentance, and a constant prayer to become more humble. However, this was only part one of the lesson I needed to learn.

Next, God began to help me understand how shaky the foundation was that I had built my self-worth upon. There are many ways this lesson could have been taught, but for me, it came as a lesson of love. First, in one ministry I was involved in, we began working our way through The Search for Significance by Robert S. McGee. I don't remember a lot about that book today, but a key concept is that many people believe a false equation—Performance plus Other People's Opinions equals Self-Worth—when the truth is that our value comes from the love and forgiveness of Jesus.

After that, during a week of revival we called a "Time of Refreshing," a pastor from a Christ Church Fellowship on the East Coast came to speak about grace. One evening that week, I had gone forward in response to the sermon. I was there with about 20 or 30 others, standing with my head bowed and eyes closed. The pastor was praying for us from the platform when he began to repeat, "I love you, I love you," over and over. Then he asked, "What is your name?" I opened my eyes to find him looking at me. "Sondra," I replied. He said, "Sondra, God loves you. He loves you. He loves you." He continued to repeat the phrase until something in me broke and I began to truly believe for the first time that God could love me personally, rather than just as a part of the collective creation of mankind.

The pastor didn't repeat this for anyone else that had responded. This was a message from God to me. Another step in this process came from a sermon in which my pastor spoke of a Hebrew word he pronounced "shamuda." The meaning of this word was "precious treasure," he taught, and was used to describe how God felt about His saints. Over time, these three truths—the love and forgiveness of Jesus, God loves me personally, I am God's precious treasure—became a solid foundation for my self-worth. However, I do want to make clear here that this transformation was actually a complete about face from the term "self-worth." I moved from the need to have worth in myself to a greater realization that I have intrinsic value as a unique creation of God and that I am deeply loved by Him. All that is good in me originates from Him and is through Him. I do not need self-promotion, but to seek to honor and glorify God alone.

After these lessons took root, I became weary. After simple attempts at getting more rest didn't lessen the weariness, I asked God what was going on. Why was I so tired and why was I not enjoying the ministries I had committed to? Jesus had said of Himself, "My yoke is easy and my burden is light." Why, then, did it feel so heavy to me at this point?

Now that my motives for ministry were purer and my foundation rebuilt on the love and forgiveness of Jesus, I was able to hear from God that the issue wasn't His yoke upon my shoulders. I had committed to most of the ministries without seeking God first. Because I was doing work intended for others, two things were happening—I was weary and I was in the way of the person God intended to do the work. I began to put each ministry before the Lord, asking if I was to continue. In the end, He instructed me to lay several of them down for others to pick up.

This was not easy. My current pastor teaches about something he calls "soul force." This is the pressure to perform according to other people's expectations and is real and tangible. A similar behavior-modifying force is commonly known as peer pressure. I found myself under significant pressure to continue everything I was doing, but I chose to obey God and lay down the weight of assignments that belonged to others. God imparted to me a functional truth that if those of us who are by nature less timid jump in to handle every ministry need, then those who are more timid will be left out. Also, just as one person could sin by not serving, I could also sin by serving. In this manner, God began to teach me of the need for seeking His will first, then committing to Him rather than to others. If I am fully committed to God first, then I will be in right alignment and true commitment to the people in my life as well.

To this day, I continue to keep watch over my desire for the limelight. It is, after all, a natural part of how God created me. It is a blessing and a strength that I have boldness and can stand in front of others. On the other hand, I have learned that with strength can come weakness. Unchecked, boldness can become domineering. Unchecked, confidence can become pride. Guarding my heart and my mind to ensure talent does not become terror is part of taking up my cross daily to follow Jesus. My desire is to become more like Him every day and He is not domineering, proud, self-seeking or self-promoting.

Did I ever receive the "Servant of the Month" award? Yes, I did—twice. The first time, I listened to the entire description of the individual without any anticipation welling up and didn't even recognize myself until my name was announced. I was surprised, but the greatest emotion was joy that God had changed me into a new person. The second time, which followed much too closely on the first, actually felt somewhat embarrassing. I believe God was showing me how much He had changed me with that one. Once again, God had proven to me that if I seek Him and His Kingdom first, He would add unto me all things.

Chapter 17
The Prayer of a Child

I love to swim. I do a lot less of it now, but while I lived in Taiwan between the ages of 10 and 13, I could almost have been described as a fish. The subtropical climate meant year-round swimming was possible, and many of my friends had swimming pools. In fact, the house we lived in for the last half of our time there also had a pool. Unfortunately, I was also very prone to ear infections. After suffering with infection followed by infection, my parents determined I should be seen by an ear, nose and throat specialist when we returned stateside for our next summer visit. During this time, flying was painful as the pressure would build in my ears, so Mom was careful to make sure I had gum to chew for every takeoff and landing.

We were able to get a referral immediately and began making the hour and a half round trip from my grandparent's home in Brown County to the ENT in Bloomington. Each visit the doctor would look in my nose, throat and ears and forcibly cause my ears to pop.

He would have me say, "K, k, k, k, k, k ..." until each ear popped. This was very unpleasant, but the ear infections were worse, so I submitted to the torture each visit. As my ears refused to improve, the frequency of the visits increased. We were on a timeline, needing to return to Taiwan, although if necessary, Mom and I would have remained behind for my medical treatment.

Eventually, we were driving to Bloomington for a daily torture treatment except for weekends. My ears continued to be stubborn and the needed healing was simply not happening. Finally, the ENT said, "We're going to have to put tubes in your ears. We'll schedule it for the day after tomorrow." At that point, my ears were sufficiently bad that he did not want me to miss a single torture session, so he made arrangements for me to see his partner the following day as the ENT was going to be unavailable.

"Does that mean I won't be able to swim anymore?" I asked.

"That's right," he said, confirming the greatest fear of my young life.

We left the office, and I was uncharacteristically quiet on the ride home, reflecting on the horrible change that was facing me. Not being able to swim felt a bit like not being able to breathe. That night, as I said my bedtime prayers, asked God for the first thing that was more than

"God bless Mommy and God bless Daddy and …." I very specifically asked God to "please just make my ears better enough that I don't need to get tubes." Then I crawled in bed and fell asleep.

The next day Mom and I headed to Bloomington again, knowing that tomorrow's trip would have a different result. I sat in the office chair, anticipating the torture treatment at the hands of a strange doctor. When he entered the room, he was pleasant enough, introducing himself and getting down to the business of looking in my nose, throat and ears. Then he looked in both ears again. He sat back for a minute and read the notes my doctor had made in my patient record. Then he looked in both ears again. Finally he sat back and said in wonder, "You're going to have to come back tomorrow. He's never going to believe me."

We had no idea what he was talking about. Of course, we were coming back tomorrow, but to the hospital for tube insertion. "Your ears are completely healed," he continued, "but he's never going to believe me, so you'll have to come back tomorrow to let him see for himself!"

My ears were healed? My ears were healed! I didn't need tubes! The doctor made a note in my chart, had the surgery appointment cancelled and changed my appointment to a regular visit the next day. We left for home, stunned and in a bit of disbelief.

The next day, my doctor skipped looking in my nose and throat and went straight for my ears! "What did you do!?" he asked. "Your ears are completely well."

"I prayed," was my response.

He then said he wanted to pop my ears one more time for good measure. I began to protest, not seeing any good reason to endure the torture if my ears were well. It turns out that "k, k, k, k" isn't the only thing that can be said to cause the popping to succeed. Apparently, protesting that popping is unnecessary also works just fine. I felt tricked, but was still elated that it would not be necessary ever again.

On the way home, although Mom was probably at least as happy as I was that the tubes were no longer necessary and that my ears were healed, she was also somewhat mystified. "You prayed," she said as she drove us home. "I've been praying for you for months."

"I guess He wanted me to ask myself," I responded with what I now recognize as wisdom beyond my years. To the best of my memory, this is the first personal lesson I received from the God of all the universe.

When we returned to Taiwan, I resumed my swimming with joy and abandon. I have not had another middle ear infection or any type of swimmer's ear since.

Chapter 18

I Am Bigger than This

When my children were young, my mother and I endured a significant period of estrangement. We had been disagreeing over what I now consider to be extremely minor issues. We each made some poor choices with regard to handling our disagreements and, in the end, Mom said to me in the church foyer one Sunday morning, "You think you can get along without me. Go ahead and try." Thus began the period of silence.

Prior to that day, we spoke on the phone nearly every day and were frequently in each other's homes. She had been up to that point a significant part of my support system with regard to juggling work, home, marriage, ministry and children (I was homeschooling as well!), and in that instant her support was pulled out from under me. After a lengthy estrangement, my father developed a significant heart issue and, while this was by no means a positive situation, it had the effect of restoring the relationship between Mom and me.

God was not in the estrangement. By this I mean He did not orchestrate it; He did not desire it; it was not His will that we be estranged. Rather it occurred out of any number of wrong and sinful choices—stubbornness, offense and pride. His word tells us that we are to live peaceably with one another insofar as it is within our power to do so. For myself, I freely admit I made choices that escalated the negativity rather than ones that could have led to peace. But God can redeem even the situations we find ourselves in as consequences of our own sinful behavior.

In the first moments following her challenge, my pride had asserted itself and assured me I didn't need my mother to help me cope with life. However, once my pride had settled a bit, I found myself wondering how and if I was going to handle life without my mother's help. Sure I had other friends, but there is something different about being able to run your thoughts, ideas, concerns and frustrations by your mother and allow her life's experiences to put your own into clearer perspective. Additionally, she was definitely my number one last-minute emergency helper. Still, I was a mother myself, and so I began to walk through each day one step at a time, accomplishing what needed to be done and continuing to spend time seeking God for strength for the day and wisdom to resolve the situation.

God soon encouraged me with a dream. In this dream, I was in the church parking lot and my mother was sitting in her car. One of the elders walked over to me, picked me up like a man would carry a bride over the threshold and carried me literally over the top of the car my mother was sitting in. For me, when the dream is detailed and the colors vibrant, I have learned that it is most likely from God rather than from my own subconscious. That was the case with this dream, so I submitted it to a close friend who is gifted in dream interpretation. The interpretation, at its most basic level, was that God, represented in the dream by the elder, was going to carry me through this situation with my mother. This revelation helped move me past the point of simply getting through each day to looking forward to each day and expecting help from God. While I continued to grieve the loss of relationship with my mother, I found that joy had returned to my life.

At that time, I was involved in a program with a group of women called 3D: Diet, Discipline & Discipleship by Carol Showalter. There were weekly meetings and assignments throughout the week. These assignments typically included both self-examination and submitting yourself to the Holy Spirit for insight into thought processes and life patterns you had developed. During one such time of self- examination and submission, God spoke to me. "You are living in the culmination of the greatest fear of your life and I AM bigger than this." I began sobbing as I instantly knew what He meant.

When I was young, probably somewhere in the 12- to 14- year-old range, my mom and I were alone in the car. We were having a conversation. I no longer recall the topic of the conversation, but I've never forgotten one sentence Mom said in the middle of it. "I only go so far with a person and then I'm done with them," she stated about herself. I had reason to believe that statement. Mom was estranged from her own parents, and her eight siblings have gone through various periods of loyalty and estrangement from each other over the years. Except for my junior year in high school when my grandfather was dying from cancer, there had not been a period during my life when everyone was on speaking terms with each other until recent years. From that moment, I had begun to fear that the time would come when my mom would be done with me. And as far as I knew in that moment when God spoke to me, my relationship with my mother was over.

"I AM bigger than this." What a comforting reality this seemingly simple statement is. At that time, I didn't know that the future held reconciliation. I didn't know that decades of relationship and fellowship lay ahead. God knew, but He didn't disclose that because He wanted me to learn a much greater truth. He is bigger than anything and everything I will face in life. He is sufficient. He is the one who supplies all my needs whether they are financial, emotional, relational or physical. God is my source. He is the great I AM and He will never fail me. The reality of that statement, the promise it held of His presence and support, and the love it implied dispelled the fear I was living with that was robbing me of joy.

I've still not forgotten what my mom said that day in the car, but it is no longer the lens through which I view my life. It has been replaced by a greater truth; a truth that is a solid foundation on which to build. "I AM bigger than this!"

Chapter 19

Baptism in the Jordan River

I love meeting with God in Israel. I have now visited Israel four times, and I long for a fifth visit. Each time I have traveled with my church family and pastor; however, the first trip was with a different pastor than the next three trips. Each trip has been remarkable, and I have learned and experienced much.

For my first trip to Israel, I went because I wanted to go. Wanting to go to Israel and experience the land chosen by God, the land that Jesus walked upon, lived and ministered in, is a good thing. And, it was a good trip with many wonderful experiences. In fact, a great deliverance occurred for me on that trip. I hadn't asked God for the deliverance I received. On some level, I probably didn't realize it was needed or available to me.

Prior to attending the church I went to Israel with on this trip, I had wasted several years as a member of a cult. I believe we are all desperately hungry for the love of God which is received through Jesus Christ, and we search to fill that hunger in many counterfeit ways until we learn of and accept Jesus as the only way, the only truth and the only life. I had been brought up to know of Jesus and had been baptized at age 12; however, I was wounded at a tender age by a few unfortunate and misguided things.

First, the church we were attending had a very definite focus on sin, hellfire and damnation. These are real issues that need to be addressed regularly, in balance, as God leads. At the church of my youth, however, no matter the scripture passage, the focus came back to sin, hellfire and damnation. I found myself at the altar week after week because I was afraid of hell. Hell deserves fear; however, fear of hell by itself is an unhealthy focus. Fear of hell was the basis for my salvation and for my baptism, but fear consumes and paralyzes rather than sustains. I thank God that He has brought me to a place of love and relationship which, while also all-consuming, brings sustenance and strength.

Against this backdrop of fear, I was told by two different men in the church that I was going to hell. The first time I was told this I was 15, and it was my pastor who told me. My mother and I had met with him as I was a member and, in this season, a leader of an organization for young girls. It was customary for the girls to attend the leader's church one Sunday during her term, and I was arranging with the pastor for that to happen. He stated that the girls could come if they wanted, but that if I did not leave this organization, I was going to hell. My mother did not refute him in the moment, but even though she did so later on the drive home, his statement remained with me. We did choose to forego inviting the girls to church.

The other man was my Sunday School teacher, a man whom I revered. I was a senior in high school, and he had asked all of the seniors in the class their plans following high school graduation. When he got to me, I stated that I planned to study Chemistry at the University of Evansville. In front of the entire class, he stated, "If you do that, you will go to hell, because you will become a scientist and scientists do not believe in God."

A short time later, I was at the University of Evansville. I had not left the young girls' organization, and I was studying Chemistry. At some level, I now knew that there was no chance for me to go to heaven, and so I did not attend church any longer. Obviously, there was no point. I was away from home and, when asked about church by my parents, I simply lied. What did one more sin matter when I was already condemned? This was the beginning of a long fall into a wayward life. I dropped out of school, married a much older man at much too young an age, and found myself living in England, pregnant with my first child and without a real support system. I was very hungry for God, and I did not want my child growing up without a spiritual foundation. Just because there was no chance for me did not mean I wanted my child to have the same ultimate fate.

While my son was still an infant, my husband and I were approached by some young men who offered a newly revealed "truth" that they were trying to help become wider known. This "truth" offered not only a path to heaven for my son, but for me as well. There was a way for me to escape hell! Without any research or prayer, we joined the cult. To be fair, there was good in the teachings of this organization. We found the other members to be kind, good-hearted people who cared about their families and the other members deeply. Unfortunately, their "truth" is simply not Truth. In hindsight, I recognize now that the Holy Spirit tried on several occasions to point out to me where the teachings did not line up with the Bible, but I suppressed His voice and continued to listen to what I was being taught.

In spite of the good family and relationship teachings of the organization, our marriage deteriorated to an alarming level. While I had accepted the teachings and joined the cult largely to ensure my son's eternal destiny, it was clear to me that he was not going to grow into a kind and responsible man unless significant change in the influences surrounding him occurred. I began to seek God for an answer, and He responded.

Even though I was on a path seeking God where He was not to be found, God knew where I was. He made it clear to me that He had released me from my marriage. I realize that will be hard for some to understand, but while I truly don't believe divorce is ever God's intended end for marriage, He wanted me out of the situation of my marriage—which was not a marriage He had planned for me—and out of the cult. Releasing me from my marriage vows was a way for both of these to happen.

By this time, I had not only a son but also a 6-month-old daughter. My parents visited England and had seen firsthand the negative situation I was in. My dad was traveling for work and arranged to fly home through England in order to help me navigate the long flight home with a toddler and an infant. The Air Force had been made aware of some of the situation and stepped in to help as well. And so, I returned to my parents' home.

My parents assisted me in returning to college and, while there, I alternated between seeking God and worrying afresh that I was destined for hell. Thoughts about the cult I had abandoned assailed me at all hours. What if they were right? If so, I had no chance to escape an eternity in the fires of hell. As the years passed, I dove into my studies, began working and began seeking a companion. Shortly before graduation, I remarried and, within a couple of months, was expecting my last baby. The pattern of seeking and fearing continued, but eventually my new husband and I began attending church with my parents. Over time, I was able to believe and eventually to know that I was on the right path and that I could indeed spend eternity in heaven with my Savior.

Still, thoughts passed through my mind from time

to time that plagued me. I now believe the thoughts were from demons either assigned to me personally or assigned to the cult I had now completely left. I would have periods of paralyzing fear, consumed with thoughts of "what if?" This was the pattern of my life, victory followed by fear followed by victory, as I left for Israel that first time.

Very early in the trip, there was an opportunity to be baptized in the Jordan River. I had been baptized at age 12 and again into the cult. Prior to leaving, I had decided that I would be baptized in Israel. It was very cold that day and there was a breeze. I waded into the water and became quite cold. However, upon my baptism, I felt extremely warm. Wet from head to toe, I stood at the side of the river in the cool breeze while the rest of the people were baptized, and yet I continued to feel warm! It was an amazing experience.

I don't believe that I know everything that happened as a result of that baptism. Certainly, there was the miracle of warmth. And while I didn't know it at the time, from that moment on, I have not been plagued by thoughts of doubt! That baptism broke the chains that the years in the cult had bound me with. I was finally free.

Chapter 20
Perfectly Healthy Heart

Several years ago, I was having some symptoms that prudence suggested a closer look by my gynecologist. Anesthesia was required, and so my gynecologist asked that I have my doctor sign off on my heart's ability to undergo the procedure. I had been experiencing what I described as familiar mild chest pain off and on but having had my heart checked out some years earlier, I was unconcerned. I had a routine visit with my primary care doctor coming up in a couple of weeks, which was plenty of time to get the required signature. So I waited until that appointment and took the paperwork with me.

Toward the end of the appointment, I told my doctor about the scheduled procedure and asked him to sign the form. "Have you been having any chest pain?" he asked. I wasn't concerned about the mild familiar pain I had been experiencing, but I always advise my patients to be honest with their physicians, and I try to follow my own advice.

"Yes, but it's the same mild pain I always have," I replied. Ultimately, he signed the form after extracting a promise from me to make an appointment with my cardiologist. By now there was a little pressure to be able to get in to see my cardiologist, who usually schedules six months out, in time for the procedure. However, when I explained the time-sensitive nature, they were able to squeeze me in with one of the nurse practitioners.

By this point, it was mid-November, and my procedure was scheduled to take place in early December. It was the first time I was seen by this nurse practitioner. She was pleasant but wasn't accepting my "I'm fine, this is all status quo" explanation of my chest pain. "Let's get an EKG just to be on the safe side," she said. "Then if that looks good, I'll sign your paperwork." By this time, it had definitely crossed my mind that I already had a perfectly good signature on my paperwork. But, I tamped my impatience down with a reminder that thoroughness is something that I value in a health care professional. And so, I submitted to the EKG, certain that everything was fine and I would soon be on my way, prepared to deal with my real health issue.

The nurse practitioner brought in the portable EKG machine and began to attach the various leads. I had wondered aloud once how they remembered which color lead attaches at what spot, and that nurse had told me they have a phrase to help them. The actual phrase has escaped my memory, but it had to do with sky over earth and smoke over fire—so blue goes above the green and black above the red—or something to that effect. It always goes through my mind during an EKG as I try to watch the leads to see if I can remember the phrase. With this in mind, I watched her, the phrase remaining elusive, and then, after typing my identity into the machine, she said, "Lie still and breathe normally." I did as instructed, the EKG machine quickly did its job, and in a few moments the leads were removed. I prepared to hear her say that everything looked fine just as I had been told so many times before.

"I want you to have a stress test," were the next words out of her mouth. I almost couldn't believe what I was hearing. That must have shown on my face to some degree, because she quickly added, "Just to be on the safe side," the second time she had said that to me. It must have been her phrase for keeping her patients from becoming anxious.

"Is that really necessary?" I asked, tamping down irritation at feeling this was all very unnecessary.

"Just to be on the safe side," she repeated. I sighed and acquiesced. I, too, often feel that in health care it is better to err on the side of caution. This particular hospital scheduled its stress tests over two days. Mine was scheduled for the Tuesday and Wednesday mornings prior to Thanksgiving. This wasn't the greatest timing, but I agreed to the dates and began to consider how to prepare for Thanksgiving with this new addition to my schedule. Then I called my supervisor to arrange to have Tuesday morning off, already having arranged to take the Wednesday off some time before.

The Wednesday before Thanksgiving, Wayne and I were resting for a few minutes before I was to begin preparing dinner when the phone rang. It was a nurse from the cardiologist's office. They had found something on my stress test and wanted to do an emergency cardiac catheterization. I questioned her about what had been found. I am well aware the nurse is not supposed to give me details, but as a pharmacist, often other health care professionals have their guard down around me and tell me a bit more than they should. She told me that the test had appeared to show several blockages before she realized what she was saying and abruptly switched course. She quickly gave me instructions for the morning of the procedure. She then asked if there was a lab open that I could get to for some lab work in preparation for the catheterization that was now scheduled for me first thing Friday morning. I told her what lab to call the orders to, having confirmed that I had just enough time to get there before they closed early for the impending holiday. Wayne and I hurried to the car, and he drove me to get my blood drawn.

Home again, I made the necessary phone calls— my children, siblings and parents all needed to know of this change in plans. My sister-in-law quickly took some of the Thanksgiving responsibilities off my shoulders. Next, I called my supervisor to let him know I wouldn't be at work on Friday. Finally, I made the most important call to my pastor to inform him and ask for prayer.

Thanksgiving was a little more strained than usual as the entire family was concerned for my well-being. However, we still enjoyed both a wonderful meal and each other's company. Friday morning found me at the hospital being prepped for the procedure. My pastor came by to pray for me. As he was praying for me, I found it very difficult to concentrate on what he was saying. This was not because of premedication—I had not yet had any— but because I was experiencing the most unusual sensation in my heart. It felt as though my heart was being gently touched by fingers. I could feel a very gentle massage of my heart. I heard my pastor say "perfectly healthy heart" as he neared the end of the prayer. I did not know what this sensation meant that I had just felt but decided I would likely know soon and just treasured the experience.

I was taken back for the catheterization. I had not met the on-call emergency cardiologist until that morning, but he was a kind and compassionate man. The experience was not nearly as comfortable as the one I had experienced about a decade earlier, but the cardiologist encouraged and comforted me as he examined the vessels in my heart. After what seemed like a very long time, he stated, "You have a perfectly healthy heart!" echoing the exact words my pastor had prayed not so long before. I was both thankful and exhausted. Wayne took me home to rest and made the phone calls to put my family and my pastor at ease. Two weeks later, I had my scheduled gynecological procedure and was told again that everything looked fine.

I had follow-up appointments with both my gynecologist and cardiologist scheduled for the same January day. My gynecologist appointment was first. "You have a pristine post-menopausal uterus!" he exclaimed, showing me pictures of a very healthy-looking organ. This, in and of itself, was a miracle. I had undergone a uterine ablation some years earlier which is a burning away of tissue. Everything should have had a charred appearance, and it should have been difficult to view clearly. In fact, my previous gynecologist had told me at a post-ablation appointment that was the case. Instead, everything was now a beautiful, healthy pink! I admit to being a bit amused by this new information. I made a follow-up appointment for the next January and went to see my cardiologist.

"What's been going on with you?" my cardiologist asked as he came into the room. He hadn't been involved in any of the cardiac appointments of the previous November. I began to describe the events, including the sensation of fingers gently massaging my heart and his colleague's pronouncement of my "perfectly healthy heart!" God had healed my heart, I concluded. My cardiologist began to downplay the possibility of a miracle as he began to pull up my chart on the computer. "Stress tests can show artifacts that can look like blockages, especially in women," he began, then said only, "Oh …" as he read the reports in my chart.

Finished reading, he turned slowly and looked directly into my eyes. "You were looking at, at least a triple bypass," he stated firmly. "Don't ever stop going to church."

"I won't," I assured him with a smile and inwardly praising God for this additional proof of what I already knew. God had opened up the vessels of my heart better and more gently than any stent or cardiac surgeon could do. And, He had done it in a very precious and intimate manner. So much love my Father has for me!

Chapter 21

A Job, A Book, A Friend

Throughout my pharmacy career, I have not always sought God with regard to whether I should change positions or career paths. However, I have learned that my job is important to Him and He will direct my path if I will ask. In fact being in the right position is imperative in order to fulfill all that He has purposed for me to do on His behalf.

The first time He spoke to me regarding my career path was during a job interview for an overnight pharmacist position at a hospital. The interview seemed to be going well, but I had not worked as a hospital pharmacist previously and I was not certain I fit the preferred candidate profile. Yet as the interview was ending, the Holy Spirit impressed upon me that I had the job. However, several weeks went by without hearing a word from the hospital. At that time, even though there were far more open pharmacist positions than there were licensed pharmacists, it seemed that I was actually not going to be offered the job. I began to question whether I had heard correctly or whether I had believed that my own preferences were the voice of God.

About five weeks after the interview, when I had already concluded that I had heard incorrectly and would not receive the job, the hospital called and offered me the position! I accepted, and on my first day working with the pharmacist who trained new staff I began to notice a trend of teasing comments being made by other staff members toward her, inquiring whether she was being kind to me. She was very nice and I was enjoying the training, so I did not really think much of it until I was asked if I planned to return as I was leaving for my lunch break. I could not think of anything I had said or done to prompt such a question, so I asked why this was a concern. As it turned out, they had offered the job to another pharmacist first who had left for lunch one day during training and called back to say she wasn't coming back because she felt the job was not for her. I had heard correctly that I had the job! It was just going to be a somewhat unusual path from interview to job offer.

Over the ensuing years, I made a number of job changes without seeking God first. However, as I came under the ministry of Pastor Jerry, I began to learn that all aspects of my life are important to God and that He wants to lead me in every area. In other words, my life is not to be compartmentalized into a job compartment that is separate from a recreation compartment that is separate from a spiritual compartment. Instead, all of my life—

career path, relationships, recreation, finance—is to be submitted to God. He is to be Lord of everything, not just what I considered to be the spiritual compartment. I began working toward submitting all things to the guidance of the Holy Spirit. I have found this to be similar to a muscle that requires exercise to remain strong, in that the more I listen and obey the guidance of the Holy Spirit the more I hear His voice, and the more I don't listen or choose to disobey His guidance the less I hear His voice.

I found myself displeased with certain aspects of the job where I was currently employed, so I began looking at job openings in the newspaper each week. One day I read a notice of a position half the distance from home to where I was currently commuting. The posted hours were significantly better—no Sundays, no late nights, short Saturdays and no holidays. And the starting salary was $10,000 more annually than my current wage. As I read the notice, the Holy Spirit told me that if I applied, I would get the position. My initial emotion was excitement, but I realized there was an "if" in what I had been told. So, expecting to hear "yes" but wanting to submit this area of my life to my Lord, I asked, "Can I apply for it?"

"No," was the surprising response.

"Are You sure?" was my knee-jerk reaction. There was a moment of silence as realization dawned on me that I had just asked God if He was sure! "I'm sorry," I added.

"Of course, You're sure. I'm the one that wasn't." It was almost as if I could sense Him smiling as I came to that moment of clarity. I put away the want ads and determined to continue with my present employment. I chose not to ask for a reason or explanation.

I was working long hours, leaving home between 6 and 8 each morning and not returning until somewhere between 8 and midnight each night. One night when I had returned home shortly before midnight, Alanna came down the stairs, burst into my room and began singing, "Hello. I love you. Won't you tell me your name?" I realized I was missing out on far too much of the last few years before Alanna entered adulthood. I already knew from God that I was not to leave this company, but I found there was an opening for a different position at work which would allow me significantly more time to spend with my family, and I made arrangements to move into that spot.

A year later God impressed upon me that He wanted me to change the hours I was working in order to be more available to Him. Generally, that is easier said than done. I was covering the night shift, and typically one cannot simply state that one now wants to work day shift and expect it to happen. Nonetheless, I made an appointment to meet with our general manager and explained to him that God wanted me on day shift. To my surprise, he had a need for a supervisor on day shift and thought I would be a good fit. Within a month, I had moved to day shift and, very shortly thereafter, was promoted to supervisor.

As supervisor, I have opportunity to meet with each of my employees individually on a regular basis, and I naturally interact with the majority of them daily. I take these opportunities to also get to know them on a personal level. Over time I came to know that one of my pharmacists, who was still a student when I became supervisor, was a Christian from Ethiopia. In fact he pastors an Ethiopian congregation and returns home most years for several weeks to hold meetings in his native country. We had a number of conversations regarding our shared belief, and I had thought that our understanding regarding being led of the Holy Spirit and the importance of obedience was similar.

One day he was expressing some concerns regarding his elementary school-aged son, and the Holy Spirit impressed upon me to give him a copy of *A Voice in the Wilderness* which is an autobiography of the life of the Rev. Loren Helm. There is an excellent chapter in the book regarding parenting which is the reason I thought the Holy Spirit wanted me to give him a copy. I mentioned the book to him, suggesting that the chapter could help him and his wife with the challenges they were facing.

Within a few days, I had given him a copy of the book. The next time we overlapped at work, he was looking for me. He had taken the book home, intending for his wife to read the chapter. Instead, she told him he should read it. As he began to read the chapter, which is not the first chapter of the book, the Holy Spirit prompted him to start at the beginning of the book. Obeying the Holy Spirit, he found that he could not put the book down! It has revolutionized his understanding of what it means to walk with God in relationship and obedience.

I then understood that when we had been speaking of things of the Kingdom, there had been a bit of a language and cultural barrier that had made each of us think we were saying the same things, when in fact there was a fair distance between our respective understanding and meaning. This pharmacist-pastor's ministry has been radically changed; he has personally distributed a large quantity of volumes of *A Voice in the Wilderness* to other pastors; and he is working with the publisher to have it translated into Amharic.

Ten years earlier, God had impressed upon me to not apply for a job that appeared better in every aspect than the job I had. And although I had not asked Him why He told me not to apply for that job, ten years later He answered that unasked question. Had I changed jobs ten years earlier, I would not have met this pharmacist. We would not have developed a Kingdom relationship, and I would have missed the opportunity for this moment of obedience that will have untold eternal significance. The thrill of this Kingdom experience far outweighs any earthly benefit that changing jobs ten years prior could have brought to me.

Chapter 22
You Know the Answer

Some time had passed following the small obedience with my Ethiopian co-worker when an opportunity for a promotion arose within the company. I had been feeling ready for the next thing in my career for quite a while at this point. This position would keep me in the same company but would move me into a separate division. This meant no loss of seniority and benefits, making this a very attractive career option. So, thinking there would be time to pray about it in the interim between application and potential interview, I applied for the position while I was on the company website.

Knowing that my immediate supervisor would be contacted to verify that I met the qualifications for transfer, I walked into his office to inform him. Before I could open my mouth, he greeted me with, "So, you are trying to leave me?!" This was my first indication that there was more urgency with filling this position than I had anticipated. In fact, the general manager called me shortly thereafter to inquire why I had not let him know I was interested in making a change. Before the day was over, the recruiter had conducted a telephone interview with me, set an appointment for a telephone interview with the hiring supervisor, and I was going with the general manager to tour the facility early the next week.

The next telephone interview went well, during which the interviewer and I discovered that, while we had never met in person, we had spoken previously and had worked together in the past. An in-person interview was scheduled within a few days to be conducted on site with the hiring supervisor and the site administrator who had to approve the final decision. I began to pray. I asked for two things: to know whether this was the right career step for me and to make a good impression in the interview regardless.

God answered my second request first. I made an extremely good impression. I found out in the interview that I had also worked very briefly with the site administrator in the past as well. We had only met once at that time but had several points of connection based upon that few weeks of overlap. I also found out that I was one of only three candidates and that the other two had not impressed either decision-maker. But I also found out some news that rattled me a bit: They wanted someone in the position by July 6 which was less than two weeks away. There was no way I could train a replacement in under two weeks, especially with a holiday in that timespan. Also, it meant I needed to hear from God very quickly regarding whether this was in His will for me.

I began praying with greater urgency. I knew I was going to receive the job offer, and I knew there were many positive aspects to the position. What I didn't know was God's will regarding the matter. Yet what happened next was also unexpected. The urgency to fill the position by July 6 became an unsettling game between corporate lawyers who were working out contracts, dollars, payment schedules and various business details, some I was privy to, some not, and some of which I probably should not have known.

I remained in my current position but began to be the unofficial liaison between the site and my current workplace as we were providing pharmacy services in the interim until the position was filled. As such, I spent hours working on reports and cost analyses and went to the site to conduct in-services for the staff that was already in place. I also was on site as a resource when the various board inspectors were there to determine if the site would receive the required licensing to open.

I began to develop a relationship with the pharmacist who held this position for a different site. She and I met for lunch a couple of times a month, discussing not only the job but also our respective children and personal lives. The hiring supervisor called me at least twice a month, keeping me abreast of the status of the negotiations to the degree that he could and encouraging me that the time would come soon for the change.

The three of us who knew about this at work agreed to keep it between us so as not to disturb the pharmacy operation in any way. We just made it known that I was serving as the pharmacy liaison to the site, and I began working on a plan for a transfer of duties. Also, knowing that it would be impossible to start a new position and immediately take an extended leave, I postponed a knee replacement that I had planned to have done before the end of the year. Thus I became heavily invested in this position, both emotionally and intellectually, long before an actual job offer was made.

During this interim, I was hearing and seeing things that concerned me professionally and personally, but I continued to work as the pharmacy liaison and to pray that God would reveal His will to me regarding this promotion. Feeling that I had not yet heard God's will in this matter clearly, I asked Wayne if he had any leading. Wayne demurred, feeling that my career choices needed to be my career choices. I counseled with my pastor who did not receive a word of knowledge for me, but he suggested that we consult with one of the elders who often heard from God on such matters. So I contacted this elder and made arrangements for him to come to our home and meet with Wayne and me. We discussed the pros and cons and prayed. Still, no definitive answer seemed to come. The elder did feel assurance that I would know God's will when the final decision was made.

In November, as I listened to a message that the hiring supervisor had left on my voicemail, I immediately knew that when I returned the call I would receive the offer. While I had not been given a salary figure, I realized that I had had months to consider whether to accept the position and it would not be appropriate to ask for time to decide. Feeling pressure to know what to do, I found a quiet place to pray. "God, I need to know what to do now," I implored. All I could feel was desperation. I was not hearing an answer. I told God that I realized I had become heavily invested and that it would be hard for me to hear clearly because of that, but surely He could break through the fog that my months of working with this facility had formed. I heard one word, a name. It was the name of a different elder. I hurried to get my cell phone and went outside to call. I had only his wife's number, but she answered and put him on the phone after telling me that he had to leave for work in a few minutes.

Realizing that time was short for both me and the elder, I quickly told him of my need for wisdom and that God had spoken his name to me. As soon as I finished, the elder stated, "God tells me that you already know the answer." As I started to respond that I did not, I realized that indeed I did know. The concerns I had been feeling were God's way of telling me that I should not take the position. A huge weight fell off me, one that I actually physically felt. I called the hiring manager, and he began to make the job offer. Interestingly, the offer had changed. It was no longer going to be a step up the career ladder but actually a rung down. I stopped him as he was about to tell me the offered salary and let him know that I would not be taking the position. He was obviously shocked, but stated that he understood.

Since that time, as I have considered the warning signals that my emotional and intellectual investment in the position had clouded, I have come to realize how blessed I am to have chosen to turn down the offer. And recently, the division was divested from our corporation. I have not heard what the ramifications of that have been for those who were already there; however, I feel certain that God led me to the correct decision for both my career and my walk with Him.

I also learned a valuable lesson about how becoming overly invested in something before hearing from God can make it much more difficult to hear from Him at all. And, I learned that He will find a way to break through if I continue to seek Him and desire His will above all else. Certainly it would have been significantly easier on me both emotionally and spiritually had I sought Him first. I am positive He would have let me know not to bother to apply.

Chapter 23

Honoring My Husband

Wayne and I are so very different in our likes and dislikes, personality types, pursuits and preferences. I am quite certain that only God would have put the two of us together. There cannot possibly be any match-making algorithm that would have determined that we were a couple likely to come to love each other, wed, and successfully navigate decades of marriage. Yet, that is exactly what happened. Still, the differences are real in both large and small ways. For instance, I strongly prefer variety and Wayne thrives on consistency.

Because I prefer variety, over the years prior to meeting and marrying Wayne, I had purchased plastic tubular hangers in a plethora of colors. In addition to basic white hangers, I had red hangers and yellow ones, orange, blue, and green hangers, and black hangers and brown ones. I had been building the hanger kaleidoscope for a number of years. At some point early in our marriage, I became aware that Wayne preferred that all hangers be only white. This was his preference. It had simply come up in conversation and there was no expectation on his part that I change anything about our hanger situation. Wayne was very aware that I enjoyed the variety of colors, and he has always wanted me to have what I enjoy.

Once I became aware of Wayne's preference, I generally tried to pay attention when I was hanging up clean laundry—choosing white hangers for Wayne's clothes and colored hangars for mine. Generally. There were times when I was simply in a hurry and paid no attention to whose clothes were going on which hanger. But there were also times when I thought that Wayne's preference was ridiculous and I would purposefully choose colored hangers for his clothes that day and, to be completely honest, I didn't try to color coordinate them either.

There came a point that our pastor's son and his closest friend—later to become our associate pastor and one of our elders—were team teaching a series on honor based upon John Bevere's book, *Honor's Reward*. If I remember correctly, our pastor was out on a sabbatical for several weeks and God had led for this important teaching. The focus over those weeks was both on honoring God and on honoring those that God places in authority in our lives, and specifically, our pastor. I recall thoroughly enjoying the series, learning much that I didn't know, and buying John Bevere's book as a result.

One afternoon as I was hanging up clothes out of the dryer with the "this is ridiculous" attitude, I reached for a brightly colored hanger with my left hand while holding one of Wayne's shirts in my right. Before I could put the hanger into the neckline of the shirt, I heard God say, "You're not honoring your husband." I was immediately convicted. The teaching that we had received over the course of several recent Sundays had prepared my heart to hear and receive that correction. I decided to make a course correction in my actions from dishonor to honor.

As a result, I purchased additional white plastic clothes hangers the next several times that I went to the store. I began a campaign to eliminate all colored hangers from our home. Every time I collected empty colored hangers from the closets, I would put them in a box that would later be donated to Goodwill. It took many months to get the majority of them swapped out. Finally, on a day that I was home alone, I did a closet raid and swapped out the rest of the colored hangers for white ones. I did forget about the coat closet and found a couple of strays in there some months later.

Funny thing is that Wayne frequently helped me with the laundry and, unless I'm doing laundry at 4 a.m. or when he's not home, he still does. Yet, he did not notice the change—not when it began, not when it was halfway done and not after the day of the closet raid. All of that effort that I made to honor my husband's hanger color preference and not one word of appreciation came from his lips. He was completely oblivious. After some time passed, I actually escorted Wayne from closet to closet to ask if he noticed anything. That worked; he realized that that our home was completely devoid of colored hangers. His response was, "You didn't have to do that."

Wayne was both right and wrong. He had no expectation that I needed to change out hangers in order for him to feel honored and peaceful in our closets. Yet, I did need to obey God and honor my husband in all ways, big and small, including hangers. To be clear, God didn't tell me to go on a colored hanger purge. That was my own idea. God simply wanted me to honor Wayne. And, the difference it made isn't in how Wayne sees me or feels about our marriage, although I imagine it has had positive effects that neither one of us is aware of, the change is in my heart and in my relationship to God.

I know that if I were to show up tomorrow with bright blue hangers for my clothes, Wayne would be fine with that. If some of his clothes were to end up on those blue hangers, he wouldn't be upset or harbor any resentment. This was never about hangers, white or colored. It was about my own personal sanctification and my ability to model through our marriage the relationship between Christ and his bride, the church.

Today, when I hang up Wayne's clothes, I specifically reach for the brightest whitest hanger available in the moment. Not because Wayne desires or expects that of me, but because it reflects the level of honor I now hold for the God-given gift of Wayne Haggard to me.

Chapter 24

God's Child

My son had made statements to me that indicated he could be suicidal. I began praying for his life and simultaneously trying to reach him via telephone, as he was living away from home, and I did not have his address. He was not answering his phone and was not at work. Finally, I was able to persuade a business that had his address on file to give it to me so that I could have the police check on him. Thankfully, he had not taken his life, and I procured a promise from him to check himself into a hospital in order to receive help and counsel. I met him at the hospital, needing to see for myself that he was going to be taken care of.

A few days later, he called from the hospital and asked that I come to visit. He requested that I bring our pastor with me. And so, my pastor and I arrived separately at the appointed time for the visit. Basically, the visit consisted of small talk, and as the allotted visiting period drew to a close, my pastor left. I remained a bit longer for another hug and, as I did so, my son handed me an envelope and asked me to wait until I got home to read it. I was not very obedient to that request but sat down on a bench outside the hospital to read the note.

The note was several pages long, handwritten, and stated that he could no longer hide from me that he was homosexual. It also stated that he understood my beliefs and would not blame me if I chose to permanently end my relationship with him, but that he needed to openly be who he was if he was to get out of the deep depression and recover his desire to live. He also stated that he had prayed for years, asking God to take these desires from him, to no avail. Thus, he had concluded that either God didn't care about him or that homosexuality was fine with God. Either way, as encouraged by the psychiatrist as a required step toward wholeness, he was informing me of his lifestyle so that he could begin healing.

So much pain was expressed in the letter and so much pain was experienced in the reading of it. My son was suffering intensely and had been for years, and I had been ignorant of it and had therefore not been able to be supportive of him or of any help or consolation in his struggle. I believe that at this point I went into shock. My first instinct was to run to him and hold him in my arms, but visiting hours were very strict and very limited; holding my child was not an option. I don't remember finding my car. I don't remember the 45- minute drive home on the Interstate. What I do remember is the very distinct impression that Jesus was sitting next to me in the passenger seat.

I did make it home safely. The first thing I did was call the hospital and ask to speak with my son which I was able to do. I told him that I loved him and that there was nothing he could do to cause me to permanently end our relationship. I was his mother; he was my deeply loved son; and that, from my perspective, was what was permanent. It was a short call with lots of tears on both ends of the phone, but I knew the first thing he needed to hear from me was assurance that my love was unchanged. I have no doubt that I needed that same assurance as well.

I called and spoke with my sister-in-law, needing support myself. I later found out that she had been forewarned, as she was the one who my son felt I would turn to. I also found out later that he had intended to tell me this in the presence of our pastor for my benefit so that I would have him for support and comfort, but he had lost his nerve and went with his backup plan which was the letter. Much later when we discussed this, he was disturbed that I had ended up driving home directly after reading the letter which was not his intent.

There was a gathering at my pastor's home that night. It was to be a cookout and a time of fellowship. I did not feel that I was in any shape to be out in public, but my sister-in-law encouraged me to not change my plans but to go. Wayne took me to the cookout, stayed by my side and took me back home fairly early. I remember nothing but numbness during that evening and through the night.

The following morning, the first thing I did was to begin to cry out to God regarding my son. As a mother, my normal thought process regarding any pain that enters into the life of any of my children consists of several concurrent ideas. What did I do wrong to cause the pain? How do I remove the pain from my child? Is there a way I can take the pain in their place? And, in the case of the pain coming from an outside source, there is the struggle to not strike out at the source of that pain. This morning, as I began to pray through the pain I was feeling and that I knew my son was feeling, I got as far as saying my son's name, "I lift up Ben…" when God spoke to me and said, "This is not your fault."

What a wonderfully sensitive thing to say to me, and how desperately I needed to hear it! Whatever side of the debate you may land on regarding homosexuality, the facts are that my son was in pain, had been in pain, and as his mother I felt in my heart that I was to blame. Feeling responsible for the pain experienced by one of my precious children has historically been a way to reduce me to ashes. God knew that, without His intervention, this was where I was headed, and He spoke truth into my heart. That truth was a healing mercy that kept me from misplacing blame onto myself. As I began letting that wash over me and bring a measure of peace, God spoke again: "And it's mine to fix." With these two statements,

God removed from me both the responsibility of causing or not preventing the pain my son was in and of finding a way to get him through it. In so doing, God showed me how well He truly knows me and what I need. He showed me that He is focused on me in every moment, and He reminded me that my son is, first and foremost, His son. Ben was entrusted to my care, but he has always been God's child.

Chapter 25
Vision of Comfort

I can't say that I did not grieve my paternal grandmother's death at the time it happened, because I did. However, there were circumstances surrounding it that likely contributed to having less than full closure. On one hand, being both a pharmacist and a granddaughter, I was involved to a degree in some of the final medical decisions. In fact, one of my clearest memories of that time is asking my mother in response to a medical question concerning my grandmother's end of life care, "Are you asking the pharmacist or the granddaughter?" She responded that she was asking both, and so she received two different answers.

While it is a tremendous privilege to be involved in the final care of a loved one, it is an equal burden. On the other hand, I was in the first year of my first job as a licensed pharmacist, and there was a lot of pressure to work through the grieving process without bereavement leave. Even though company policy included the typical three days off, the company was fairly new to Indiana with no relief pharmacist pool established, so when I called my district manager with the news that my grandmother had passed away, his response was, "Good luck finding your own relief." Therefore, I found myself at work the morning after her passing, trying to accurately fill prescriptions through intermittent tears while also making phone calls to sister pharmacies trying, without success, to find pharmacists willing to work a shift or two for me.

After a couple of hours and a number of phone calls, a district manager who managed a neighboring district heard of my situation, called to tell me that he would handle it from that point and sent one of his pharmacists to relieve me for the remainder of that shift. Finally, this was not a point in my life that I was truly walking with the Lord, so while I felt assured of Grandma's eternal destination, I was not so sure of my own. My grandmother's pastor was the same one who had told me I was going to hell as a child, so the service itself did not provide significant peace. Thus, I did not have the comfort of anticipating a final and eternal reunion.

Some years later, I was attending church with my parents regularly and my walk with the Lord was growing. The church had three praise and worship teams and, although my initial reaction to praise and worship had been concern bordering on fear, I had learned to embrace the intimacy of abandoning myself to worship God through music. It is through praise and worship that I learned I can sing. I had been told as a child that I could not sing and would never be able to. That was a horrible weight for me to bear as I loved music. However, when I praised God in song, I wasn't worried about how I sounded; I simply poured my love for Him out through song. Over time, I had people tell me I should try out for a part in the church Christmas musical, and eventually this led to me being a part of two different praise teams. To this day, praise and worship remains one of the greatest pleasures in my life.

I believe that a great part of my love for music was instilled by my grandmother. Throughout most of my life, she was the song leader for her church. As such, she chose three hymns with which to begin each service and would then choose the invitation hymn that most closely aligned with the sermon for the end of service. She would go to the front of the church and announce the hymn number from the hymnal and then lead the congregation in singing it. Typically, she would lead us to sing the first, second and fourth verses. Singing the third verse was very rare. In fact, I was an adult before I heard the third verse of "How Great Thou Art" which is probably the most moving verse of the song.

On Wednesday nights, she often let me choose the songs with her. There were many, many Wednesday night services that included "Love Lifted Me" as that was a favorite hymn of mine at the time. Only rarely would Grandma suggest that perhaps we should choose a different song that Wednesday night.

Grandma had also sung in a large women's choir, but I believe that to have been either when I was very small or before I was born, as I don't recall anything but occasional mentions of it having happened. Occasionally there were special songs—solos or duets—that the congregation as a whole would not sing. My grandmother was often, though not always, the soloist or a part of the duet. Much to my chagrin at the time, there were a couple of occasions when she enlisted me to be a part of the duet. I recall many times that she would choose to sing "The Old Rugged Cross" during the Christmas season. She nearly always explained first that, while most people would consider it to be more appropriately sung at Easter, it was for the cross that Christ was born.

Over the years, God has frequently chosen to speak to me through song, sometimes even through a line or two of a secular song. This particular occasion was during a Sunday service several years following my grandmother's death. At this church, services were begun by announcements and prayer by an elder. Next was 30 minutes of praise and worship, followed by communion and the offering. There might be a time of testimony and/or prayer requests, then the sermon, and finally a time of ministry. The praise and worship typically followed a pattern beginning with upbeat praise songs and ending with more reflective worship songs. The praise team had concluded the more upbeat part of the worship segment and began to lead the congregation in "The Old Rugged

Cross." I was singing along with the very familiar and memorized song. The praise team was on the platform, and I was surrounded by some 300 other worshippers.

Suddenly yet peacefully, that all changed. In place of the praise team, there was Grandma. She was wearing a very familiar blue print dress with a matching fabric belt at her waist, and she was leading the singing of "The Old Rugged Cross." The congregation remained around me but became very indistinct. As I watched Grandma continue to lead the song, her blue dress changed into a dazzlingly white robe and, still singing, she ascended into heaven. As she went through what had become a church ceiling that was open to the sky, the ceiling reformed, the congregation came back into focus, and the praise team concluded the song.

To the best of my memory, this was the first vision I had experienced and its purpose was multifold. I may still not know all that this vision accomplished; however, first it introduced to me another way that God is able to speak to me. It gave me great closure and even greater comfort. I later shared it with my father and, while he isn't prone to sharing his feelings, I believe it was a great comfort for him as well. Also, it was a moment of intimacy with my Grandma. There have been a number of times since that I have been able to sense her as a part of the great cloud of witnesses when I have been praising God in song. In fact, I am writing this chapter today largely because yesterday was one of those days.

It is truly a blessing to have the knowledge that she is one of the saints praising God in His throne room and that there are times we still sing together. Greater still is the knowledge that we will praise our Heavenly Father together for eternity.

Chapter 26

A Joyful Giver

Shortly after I returned to my faith in God, I determined to begin tithing. It certainly wasn't a decision made because I had so much extra money that I felt I could afford to tithe, for that was certainly not the case, but simply that I wanted to begin being obedient in this area.

Initially I wasn't a joyful giver, but I was a committed one. As I said, I determined to tithe. After conferring with my husband, I began by giving 10 percent of our net income to the penny. There were weeks when that seemed impossible, but I gave and, week after week, our bills were met. After some time, I increased our giving to 10 percent of our gross income. Again, some pay periods were more difficult than others, and while there was sometimes stress related to writing that check, it was written faithfully. I became a faithful giver, and although I didn't smile inwardly or outwardly while I wrote the checks nor when actually placing them in the offering, I didn't begrudge it either.

Several years after I began tithing, the church held a conference which was attended by approximately 800 people. During the afternoon session of one of the days of the conference, the speaker stated that there would be an offering that evening. He instructed us to ask God what amount we should give in that offering. This was a new thought for me. To this point, I believed that tithing was 10 percent of income and that was the prescribed dollar amount. Anything over and above that for special offerings was based upon availability of funds. If I had extra and wanted to give, I did. If not, I didn't.

I wanted to obey the speaker's instructions. During the break between the afternoon and evening sessions, I asked God to reveal the dollar amount we were to give. Remarkably, my husband and I agreed upon the amount. It was not a comfortable amount and would require some adjustments. But, I wrote the check and took it with me to the evening service. I was scheduled to serve on the ministry team that night, being available for prayer at the conclusion of the session. This meant that I was to sit on the front row so that there would be no delay in my availability.

The session opened with prayer and a time of praise and worship. Then the afternoon's speaker took the platform and announced that it was time for the offering. He asked if God had revealed to us what we should give, and there was a murmur of agreement throughout the room. He then instructed that we should give it cheerfully, as God loves a cheerful giver. At this point, while I wasn't a reluctant giver, I was certainly not a cheerful giver. Instead, I was a determined, faithful, obedient giver. I could have been described as a lawful giver. A slight panic began to arise in my heart as he went on to say that if we could not give the amount God had instructed cheerfully, we should not give it at all.

The speaker began to pray over the offering, and I began to pray as well, pleading with God to help me to be a cheerful giver. In that moment, I wanted to give the amount He had told me to give, but I wanted to do it because He said so. The amount pinched. I was determined to give it, but I wasn't necessarily happy about it. The prayer ended and the praise team began the songs that would be the backdrop for the offering. I was on the front row and the offering plate was going to be in front of me very quickly. Could I give it cheerfully?

Suddenly I began to giggle. In the minute or so that it took the offering plate to get to me, the giggle turned into a laugh. Feeling pretty cheerful, I placed the check into the offering plate and the laughing intensified and grew louder. There were 800 people singing at this time, so my laughter was not noticed except by those immediately beside me. I continued to laugh. And, I continued to laugh. I don't know how long it took to collect that offering. I do know the praise team led more than one song as I continued to laugh nonstop throughout the entire offering. At some point, I became concerned that I would be unable to stop laughing and would have to step outside so that my laughter would not be a disruption when the music stopped. I felt quite unable to stop the laughter myself; it was bubbling up and out of me from somewhere I did not recognize.

The offering was completed, and the music stopped. The laughter stopped in the same moment! I was able to stay in the service and listen to the teaching without being a distraction, although I admit to musing over my experience throughout the remainder of the evening. That was the first and, to this day, only time I have personally experienced holy laughter, although I have witnessed others having the same experience. God began a work in my heart that night during that offering.

Since that night, I have become a cheerful giver. Not only that, but from that point and over time, I have learned to give according to revelation rather than law. In other words, my "tithe" is no longer 10 percent nor is it some other percent that I calculate. Instead, it is a dollar amount that God reveals to me to be His will for my giving. He changes the amount from time to time, typically increasing it, but once He actually decreased it for a set period. It is currently greater than 10 percent of my income, but that is not the point. It is simply the amount He wants me to give.

It still pinches sometimes, but I smile when I write the checks, always inwardly and sometimes outwardly as well. I look forward to the offering as a form of both worship and obedience. I want to give to Him. I have found it pleases both of us.

Chapter 27

Called to Love

My family was less than enthusiastic when Wayne and I announced our engagement. I understand many of the reasons. I was already twice divorced. I had three children who would be affected by the change. And against what even I would typically advise, we met, became engaged and married extremely quickly. Twenty-one years later, my family loves and appreciates Wayne and recognizes the love and stability our marriage represents. However, at the time, my sister and her husband felt strongly that they could not support our decision to marry and, because of that, chose to not attend the wedding and reception. To be sure, their decision caused us some pain, but we were married nonetheless, and our ceremony and reception were still filled with love and joy.

At some point in the last 21 years, my sister, Leanne, and her husband came to regret their decision. At some point, we had forgiven them. However, neither of us ever spoke of it. We knew we had forgiven them; they knew they wished they had chosen differently. We saw each other at major holidays. We prayed for each other's families. We spoke occasionally on the phone. We each lived out our busy lives. It seemed enough to both couples. We were family, after all, and we knew we loved each other.

During those years, Ben had entered into a serious relationship and moved from Texas to California to live with a man that he described as someone who was building him up emotionally in ways that he had previously been beaten down. While I was happy that Ben had someone who recognized his value and was helping him to recognize it as well, it was still difficult for me to accept my son was living as a homosexual. Complicating matters was the fact that I had not met this man, and when we did finally meet for the first time, it did not go well. Edward knew my beliefs and came to meet Ben's family expecting to be treated poorly and kept his guard up, not wanting to be open to attack or pain. And so, while I didn't dwell daily on the situation, I did pay attention as various states legalized same-sex marriage, dreading but fully expecting the day California would follow suit. Sure enough, that day came.

From that point, I expected to receive an engagement announcement. I didn't know what I would do once it came, but I remained steadfast in loving my son with all my being. When the call came, the timing was not at all optimal. I was scheduled to have a total knee replacement of my right knee exactly six weeks prior to the date of the wedding which was to be held in Las Vegas. I had no idea if I would be able to travel that distance without first consulting with my surgeon. Ben knew about my surgery, but in his excitement had not remembered to consider that when setting the date. Additionally, while he truly wanted me there, he had no expectation that I would come. I told him that I would check with the surgeon and let him know whether I would be able to attend.

After the call with Ben, I called my associate pastor to pray with me. I not only needed to have travel clearance from my surgeon, but I also needed to have God's wisdom in the matter. I knew that this decision, and truly all decisions, needed to be made based upon His will. At the end of the prayer, I knew that I would hear from Him soon. The surgeon told me there should be no reason I couldn't travel and gave me some instructions to follow. And very quickly, God told me to go. In fact, He was very specific. He told me that I was not to inflict the same pain upon my son that had been inflicted upon Wayne and me at our wedding. We were to attend and do so out of love. I had great peace with that answer. Loving my son is not a chore or a burden; it is simply reality. So I called Ben to let him know we would be attending and began to make flight arrangements.

Almost immediately I caught a cold that caused me to lose my voice. While I had no voice, Leanne called me urgently. She said that she and Michael wanted to discuss something important with me, but she would call back in a few days when my voice returned so that I would be able to carry my part of the conversation. When we spoke a few days later, after ascertaining that I felt better, her first comment was to tell me that I was not to make the same mistake with Ben that she and Mike had made with Wayne and me. She said that if I didn't go to the wedding, I would never be able to undo that decision. I stopped her and explained that God had already told me the same thing, that Ben knew we would be there, and that I already had the airplane tickets and accommodations arranged. The relief in her voice was unmistakable. We had such a wonderful conversation from that point, expressing regret, extending forgiveness and becoming clear with one another.

I learned the truth about the importance of clarity in relationships that day. We could have continued to muddle through our relationship until the end of our respective lives, but the new closeness that expressing to each other what we thought and felt, extending apologies, forgiveness and mercy to one another is so much greater! My love for my sister has grown exponentially because of one conversation where we each expressed what had been on our hearts for years.

And so, my knee was replaced, and I began physical therapy with the goal of being able to maneuver through Las Vegas well enough to not cause any concern for the rest of the wedding guests and, more importantly, for Ben and Edward. While the majority of my concentration was on the new knee, as the date of the wedding drew closer, I would have moments of stress wondering what my personal reaction would be to the ceremony. Each time that happened, I would take it to God. Each time, He assured me He would be with me. Each time, I felt peace return.

The date arrived to board the plane for Vegas. We were arriving the Wednesday ahead of the wedding and leaving the Wednesday after. We were able to spend time with Ben and Edward as they showed us around Las Vegas which is a city they particularly enjoy. This was time during which we were truly able to begin to see Edward in a new light. We were also able to meet and spend some time with Edward's family when they arrived a couple of days after we did. I had not quite met my goal of causing no concern regarding my physical state, but considering that Ben is very solicitous of me, I probably came as close as possible considering I was only six weeks post-surgery.

The morning of the wedding arrived. I had purchased a new dress shortly before receiving the wedding announcement, and I had reserved it to be worn for the first time that day. Every time that a doubt attempted to creep into my mind, I heard God reassure me that He was with me. We arrived at the venue and waited to be admitted. Wayne and I, Diona and Alanna were there for Ben. Leanne joined via Diona's cell phone. Alanna's future husband, Will, joined by cell phone as well. And God was there with me just as He had promised. He kept my focus on the things that would bless my mother's heart. What I saw was not two men entering into a same-sex marriage, although that is, in fact, what occurred. Instead, God showed me the joy on Ben's face. God showed me the love in Edward's eyes. And God began to fill my heart with love for this man, Edward, who is now my son-in- law.

God reminded me again that day of my responsibility, my role, my calling. I am not responsible to deliver Ben or Edward from homosexuality. It is not my role to judge or to condemn. I cannot throw the first stone at anyone because I have not lived a life without sin. I cannot do anything about my own sin, much less anyone else's. Only Jesus can bear that. It is, however, my responsibility to love. I am to love God before all else and to seek Him and His kingdom first and foremost. In addition, as a wife and a mother, it is my role and a significant part of my calling to love my husband and my children. As a Christian, I am called to love as Jesus loves and who He loves. He loved me when I was unlovable and long before I loved Him. I am seeking to love like that. And, I am finding that love only multiplies. It does not divide.

Chapter 28
The Sweetest Voice of All

I have been learning that it is of utmost importance to be vigilant regarding the fact that there are always voices that compete with God's voice. Often those voices are the loudest and seem the most familiar. I have found there are basically four sources that try to sway me to action apart from God—self, family and friends, the world, and the enemy. The first two, generally speaking, have a vested interest in my well-being but may not be speaking from an awareness of God's purposes for me, and the second two have no concern for me whatsoever. These four voices can seem more real, more compelling and even more logical than the voice of God.

My own voice—thoughts, ideas, goals, plans—is a constant. I want to succeed in life—career, finances, family, friends—and so, to that end, I have my best interests at heart. I plan to go to work each day and accomplish my best there. I hope for a measure of recognition and promotion. I desire financial stability.

And, I want to share love with my family and

friends, both as a giver and as a recipient. There is nothing unusual or inherently wrong with any of that. However, the path I think is the best way to obtain that is often not the path God would have me walk. While my plan may be good, His plan is always best. Therefore it is imperative that I seek Him and His purposes first before I commit to any plan or action. Also, I need to remain open to interruption at all times. I don't need to ask God each day if I am to go to work. I can start with the assumption that I am to go to work each day. However, if God tells me something different on a given morning, I need to be prepared to change direction.

My family and my friends care about me. They want me to be generally happy, healthy and relatively solvent. So when I receive advice or direction from them, I know they have my best interests at heart. However, while it is important to listen to them with respect, it is even more important to consider whether they are advising me based upon their own accumulated wisdom or whether they are speaking God's heart to me.

Another consideration with my family and friends is to resist pressure. Family traditions are not inherently bad, but God may want me to be somewhere different on a given holiday. The assumption that I will fall in line with holiday, vacation or birthday plans is a very persuasive form of pressure, and it is much easier to cave in to it than to stand against it. Recently I enjoyed a wonderful Thanksgiving with my family, but there was a previous year when God's plan was for Wayne and me to be in Israel on Thanksgiving. It would have been easy, but wrong, to tell God we couldn't go to Israel because we needed to be with family on the holiday.

The world is a great distraction that appeals to my desires. Advertisements bombard me from all directions, promising contentment, satisfaction, adventure and a host of other positives if I go, do or purchase. Television, radio, billboards, newspapers and magazines all try to create needs and desires I didn't even know I had a moment before. The allure and enticements are creative and, all too frequently, successful. I can find myself pursuing a dream that was created by a stranger whose goal is to lighten my wallet while fattening his own. It is entirely too easy to end up in a bondage of debt that prevents me from pursuing the dreams that God has given me. In addition to that, the world encourages a lifestyle that seeks power and fame, frequently through manipulating and harming others. If what I am about to do is detrimental in any way to another person, it is highly unlikely that I am on the path God wants me to walk.

The final competing voice—that of the enemy—can sometimes be the most difficult to discern. The strange thing is that when God speaks to me, there is a tendency to wonder where that thought came from, while when the enemy speaks it often seems as though it is my own thought. The enemy is wily and understands human nature and thought patterns. And, while God is a gentleman and always plays fair, the enemy does not.

The enemy is the father of lies, to be sure, but he often uses a tiny piece of truth as the bait on his hook. As an example, my personality is such that I don't cry easily, and I don't tend to fall apart in emergencies. I take care of what needs to be done in the moment and, when everything and everyone has been cared for, I may grieve then, typically alone. For instance, my grandfather passed away days after I gave birth to my firstborn. I was living in England and had been through a Caesarean section. My parents chose to wait to inform me of my grandfather's passing until I was home from the hospital. At that point, the funeral had already occurred. I was physically unable to fly home and, while I experienced a moment of grief, I took care of recuperating from the surgery and loving and caring for my son. It was more than a year later that I pulled out the ribbon my mother had sent me embossed with "great grandfather" and grieved my grandfather's death while Ben slept.

The enemy began to speak to me about this. He would get my focus on another person who wept easily while I was not even close to tears. Then he would whisper to me that I was cold-hearted and uncaring. The bait on the hook, the sliver of truth, was that I don't cry easily. The barb, the painful debilitating lie, was that I was cold-hearted and uncaring. I believed this lie about myself for more than a decade before I listened to the healing voice of God as He gave me His perspective about myself.

He made me to be strong in order to minister to others in times of distress. Holding it together and helping others is the way I demonstrate caring; making myself available is the proof that I am not cold-hearted.

I have a tendency to listen to that sliver of truth when I hear it and then swallow the hook and run with it, allowing it to embed itself deeper and deeper into my self-identity. Satan may whisper that I'm a failure, uncaring, a loser, a bad parent, unforgiveable, and I answer back with, "Yes, yes, tell me more" when I should instead take all of that to Jesus.

The truth is that we all fail and we all sin, but Jesus has paid the price and, when we take it to Him in repentance, it is wiped off our slate and we are pure and holy before God. God wants us to grow more and more like Him as we walk through our lives. We cannot do this by agreeing with the enemy's lies about our identity, but only by continuing to submit our words, thoughts, emotions and actions to our Creator who knows exactly who we are and who He created us to be.

The enemy condemns and the Father convicts. I have a friend who gave me an illustration that has helped me to recognize which is occurring in a given moment. Picture yourself in an empty room. The room has no light, no windows, and is a cluttered mess. You are locked in the dark room and told to clean it up. That is condemnation. Now picture the same room. You are in the same dark and cluttered room, but the Holy Spirit comes into the room, turns the lights on and says, "Let's get this cleaned up." That is conviction.

What I personally try to do now when the enemy accuses me of a sin or failure is respond in a way that glorifies God and doesn't trash His creation—me. If it is from my past and I have already taken it to God and it is therefore already forgiven, I praise God and thank Him for His provision, His love and His forgiveness. If it is a current failing, I confess it to God for forgiveness and ask Him to cleanse me and help me to change. If it is a character trait, I ask God to show me His perspective. It may be that God sees that character trait in a completely different light.

I don't always get this right the first time, but as God continues to work in me and as I continue to seek Him, I grow more like Him and hear His voice more clearly. That's the voice I really want to hear and listen and respond to. The voice of the lover of my soul is the sweetest voice of all.

Chapter 29

The Power to Choose

Yesterday morning as I prepared for the day, I looked at myself in the mirror. That is obviously not an unusual occurrence. But, this particular morning, as I looked at myself, a memory of a former pastor saying something to me that likely should not have been said crossed my mind. For many years, this was something I had nursed in my heart in a list of grievances regarding this pastor. However, earlier this year, he was most definitely on the list of people I had forgiven in the wonderful miraculous and healing session of forgiveness the Holy Spirit had taken me through. How then, you might wonder, would this memory return at this time?

I don't know if the memory was simply that—a memory I happened to recall at that moment. The comment was specifically about my face which was being reflected back to me in the mirror, so that would certainly be a possibility. It is also possible the enemy whispered it into my ear in an attempt to rob me of the victory of forgiveness that had been won. Regardless, as I realized the wrong direction my thoughts were beginning to take, I arrested the thought and stated, "No! I have forgiven this pastor and I have specifically forgiven him for this statement. I am not going to review it."

I may not have the power to prevent a thought from crossing my mind, but I do have the power to choose what to do with it. I can dwell on it and allow unforgiveness to creep back in, or I can take the thought captive and remind myself of truth. The same is true of other types of thoughts. I may not be able to prevent the thought that someone looks attractive to enter my mind, but I choose whether to simply appreciate the beauty that God has created and move on, or I choose to dwell on it which can lead to lust. Many thoughts are not inherently sinful, but what we choose to do with those thoughts absolutely can be.

Having refused to allow the negative thought to move from thought to thought pattern, I then stated that it is not my place to judge. Only God can truly judge the intent of the heart. At that point, the Holy Spirit began to teach me. He explained that I was also not in the place of defense attorney. That truth was pretty simple for me. Jesus is our advocate before the Father, so in this allegory, He would have the place of defense attorney. Next the Holy Spirit stated that I also do not have the role of prosecutor. My only role is to offer forgiveness as I have also been forgiven by my Father because of the sacrifice of Jesus. Again, as this is something I have already walked through, it was an easy lesson for me to absorb.

A moment passed and the Holy Spirit spoke again. "When you choose unforgiveness and continue to rehearse the wrongs you have suffered, you take a place that is also not yours. Unforgiveness and rehearsing of wrongs puts you in the place of the accuser." This was a much bigger truth to absorb. If I choose not to forgive, I take on the role of the accuser. If I rehearse—mull over, complain about, discuss—acts that either have wronged me or that I have perceived to have been wrong, I am putting myself in the role of the accuser. Under no circumstances do I want to align myself with satan, the accuser. This has given me even greater resolve to choose forgiveness quickly and to refuse to rehearse and nurture wrongs, whether large or small.

As I have reflected on this since yesterday morning, I also see the love and care that God has for me in that He taught me this in a moment of victory. Choosing this timing made the lesson a blessing, and it lifted me even while I realized more fully the depth of the pit that unforgiveness truly is. Had the same lesson been expressed to me in a moment of failure, it would have been no less true and the gravity would have been no less, but it would also have been painful.

How great is the love of our Father that He wants us fully restored into His image! How tender is He that He does not bruise us as He transforms us to become more like Him! He takes such care in every detail of our sanctification, and since He knows us so intimately, He is perfect in his timing.

Chapter 30

A Deer Encounter

For many decades, one of my heart's desires has been to have a husband who prayed with me. I have long known that Wayne prays for me and that has been a tremendous blessing and comfort, but he is a generally quiet man whose natural inclination is to listen rather than to speak. Praying is not a challenge for him, but praying out loud, even when it is only in front of me, has been quite a challenge.

A number of years ago, our church purchased some property with the intent to build our first permanent building. Until now, and as I type this is still the case, we have moved from one temporary meeting place to another as God has led and provided. Many of these places have required both setup and teardown each week. God has met with us and blessed us in each venue and, while the extra setup and teardown effort is sometimes wearing, it has also had the effect of binding many of us closer together. Nonetheless you can imagine our excitement and anticipation regarding having a building of our own

Sondra Leigh Haggard

for worship and ministry!

Building projects are never without their roadblocks and delays, and ours is no exception to that. A few years ago, God led for us to have a 40-day period as a congregation dedicated to prayer regarding our building program. The areas of prayer focus were fourfold. First, we were to pray for God to get us to our next interim meeting space where we could have room to grow. Second, we were to ask for an increase in commitment, obedience and love. Third, we were to pray for breakthrough in the construction process. Finally, we were to pray that the "keys" to helping us in the building process would be both in place and engaged. We were to ask God, as individuals or family units, how He would like that to be accomplished through us. God asked Wayne and me to commit to going physically to the church property twice a week to pray there. We committed to do as He directed and began going every Monday and Thursday evenings when I got off of work. When both the lateness of the hour and the weather allowed, we would walk the property as we prayed.

The first week, I took the lead in prayer, but it wasn't long before we were taking turns fully and praying as a team. By the end of that 40 days, it was no longer difficult for Wayne to pray out loud in front of me! To my surprise, Wayne's new freedom in prayer also affected how free I felt to pray in front of him. I had not realized that I was holding back myself, either because of my own

168 | P a g e

discomfort or in an attempt to not increase his discomfort, or perhaps a combination of both. We began to discuss continuing to go to the property twice weekly when we were told that God had led for us to have a second 40 days of congregational prayer. God was already preparing us to continue.

During this second 40-day period, Wayne and I were walking on the property one evening praying out loud. The property is a beautiful lot, the front road access side being largely cleared, but still containing several beautiful mature trees. There is a large wooded area through which a path has been created, and the back is bordered with a large, flowing creek. We have eagles nesting on the property that many of us have been blessed to see, and you can often hear horses neighing from our neighbor's property across the creek. We were walking on the path through the wooded area when I heard the sound of a stick being stepped on behind me. Assuming someone else had joined us to pray on the property, I turned to see who was there. It was not another member of the congregation behind us. I told Wayne very quietly to turn around slowly to look. About 10 yards behind us, watching us, were two beautiful young bucks! They just had about an inch of antler growth. We stood still as they walked up to us. Wayne was a bit closer to them than I, and the first of the bucks walked right up to him and nudged his hand with its nose the way a dog would do to encourage petting. So, Wayne reached out and began petting the deer! Over the course of the next 15 or 20 minutes, Wayne and I both were able to pet each deer, and I finally had the presence of mind to take a few pictures to prove it!

Not only were we petting the deer, but we began to continue praying out loud, thanking God for the experience and the beauty of His creation. I also began to sing praises to God. Throughout all this, the deer remained with us. After this petting session, Wayne and I continued to walk and pray. The deer continued watching us and, when we turned around to walk back toward our car, the deer came up to us again and another petting session ensued!

One of the repeated prayers we had been praying over the property was that it would be a safe place, a haven for the wounded and a place of healing. How safe a place is it when two deer, which are likely among the most wary and skittish of God's creatures, walk up to two humans and request to be petted? I believe at least two things were happening that evening. My pastor has said many times that animals respond to the presence of the Kingdom of God. I believe the Kingdom was present as we were praying and the deer were responding to Him. I also believe God was letting Wayne and me know that our petition—that the church property would be a safe haven—was being heard and was a correct petition, one that is from the heart of God for the property.

Eighty days of prayer as a congregation for our church property and eighty days of obedience from this household—it was really a small period of time in the greater scheme of things, but in this household, it resulted in tremendous blessing. Wayne and I pray together regularly and are comfortable doing so. Our marriage, which was already good, is even stronger and more intimate. I have received my heart's desire of a husband who prays with me. And, we got to pet, pray and praise with two deer!

Chapter 31

Quiet Faith

As mentioned before, my husband is a man who listens much and talks not so much. This remains a very dramatic difference between the two of us and was especially so early in our marriage when I talked enough for both of us and probably used an additional person's word allotment on most days. Over the years, we have each moved a bit toward the middle ground, but Wayne easily continues to be the listener and I the talker of the marriage.

I can talk about most any topic, but I do have some clear favorites. First and foremost, I enjoy talking about my God and Savior and what He has done, is doing or will be doing. Next, I do enjoy talking about my children and my husband. God and my family are sources of great joy in my life. I also deeply love my church family and will frequently find myself talking about them. Finally, my chosen vocation of pharmacy is a deep passion of mine. So in the first year of our marriage, I would talk with Wayne about God daily. He was already a Christian when we met, so talking of things of the Kingdom with him was natural to me. Wayne listened and listened but rarely responded with his own observations.

As we moved into our second year of marriage, I was not talking any less to Wayne, but I had begun sharing things of God with him a bit less frequently. My passion for God was no less, but the lack of response from Wayne was a bit like cold water in the middle of a warm shower to me. So, I was sharing more with our new church family and less with Wayne.

Looking back, I don't recall a conscious decision on my part to slow down the sharing. I believe that I simply received a more encouraging response from my Christian friends than from my husband. Also, without realizing it, I made an assumption that Wayne wasn't hearing from God and that's why he had nothing to share with me. I didn't love Wayne any less, although I was very likely on a slippery slope at that point, but I was allowing his natural tendency to listen and process inwardly, rather than to speak and process outwardly, to send me in a very wrong direction.

We attended Wednesday night church services on a regular basis during this time but came from two different directions to get there, so we were always in separate vehicles. On the drive home, there was no stated or unstated rule about which vehicle would lead, and on this particular night, I happened to be in the lead. At one point, I looked at Wayne in my rearview mirror and, as I did, I heard, "I speak to Wayne, too."

I don't believe I actually said, "What?!" out loud, but the question definitely crossed my mind.

"I speak to Wayne, too," God repeated.

With that simple statement, God corrected significant wrong thinking I was entertaining about my husband and changed the course of our marriage. In the car on that drive home, I repented of thinking of myself as more spiritual than my husband. I repented of allowing seeds of disrespect toward him to be sown. I repented of choosing to share with others in place of my husband.

The reality is that it took a number of years for Wayne to begin sharing more with me, but I suspect it would never have happened at all if I had not chosen to repent and to respect his differences. To be fair, it has also taken years for me to learn that not every thought that passes through my mind needs to exit through my mouth. Even today, we could each still move a bit more toward the middle, but I am so thankful God not only put us together, He also corrected me when I was moving off course. Without God's intervention, our marriage would likely be much different than the strong and beautiful relationship it is today.

Chapter 32

God Speaks through Dreams

Wayne is a dreamer. By that I mean two things. He dreams big dreams for things he would like to own or build or do, but also God speaks to him in dreams frequently. God also speaks to me in dreams, and while it hasn't happened frequently, one of my favorite things is when God speaks to both of us in a dream about the same topic.

The June following the 80 days of prayer for the church property was one of the times that happened. When we had both awakened, Wayne began to share with me a dream he had regarding the deer we had petted on the church property. In this dream, we had continued going to the church property on Mondays and Thursdays to pray, but we had begun to take corn with us to feed the deer. Over time, the deer grew and had families. They began to bring their young ones to meet with us. Over the same time interval, we increased our commitment to prayer on the property and began going on Tuesdays and Fridays as well. On Tuesdays and Fridays, the eagle would show up. So we began bringing mice for the eagle and Wayne wore protective sleeves. The eagle would land on Wayne's arm and eat the mice. It was a messy process. Each animal knew which days of the week to come to be fed. The deer came only on Mondays and Thursdays and the eagle only on Tuesdays and Fridays.

As I listened to Wayne, I grew quite excited. When he finished, I told him that I had also dreamt of the deer that night. In my dream, we had taken Alanna with us to the property to pray and had brought corn for the deer. Apparently some time had passed, as the deer had grown both taller and fatter. They were a little skittish at first but then seemed to realize who we were. One of the deer had a rope around its neck. The deer without the rope came to us first and played with us and ate corn. Then the other deer came to me. I was gentler and less playful with this deer, petting him and reassuring him. The deer did not like it when I touched the rope, but began to eat corn from my hands and Alanna's hands as well. Wayne was then able to cut the rope from his neck.

I have had dreams from God that are very literal, but most often they are symbolic. In other words, I do not expect to actually participate in feeding mice to the eagle on the property, but I do believe that we will be ministering to people who attend our church once we begin meeting on the property. I believe the dreams speak to God's plans for the property, for Wayne and me, and for those He brings to us there. Interpretation of dreams is not a typical part of my spiritual skill set—I think that's one reason God often gives me more literal dreams—but there is much more I believe I know about these dreams. And, I am also certain there is much I do not yet know.

The fulfillment of these dreams is yet to come, as they clearly speak of a future time. It is possible from the dreams that some of the fulfillment is contingent upon our continued, and perhaps increased, commitment to our roles in the church body God has placed us in. Regardless, we are both looking forward to see all that God has planned for us and for our church.

Yet how good is God! In the second year of our marriage, he corrected my thinking about my husband when I was veering in a wrong direction. More recently, He worked in us over the course of 40 days, and then 40 more, to bring us to a place where praying together became natural. Without God's involvement in our marriage, we would not have the type of relationship that He can use in this manner.

God truly prepared this man for me, but not just for me. Our marriage is intended to be used of God for His purposes. Over the course of our marriage, He has been continually preparing and shaping us to that end.

I love Israel. The times I have spent in that country are among the highlights of my life. God has been so faithful to meet with me in so many wonderful ways when I have sought Him in the land where Jesus walked the earth. It is a rare day that I am not longing to return there and anticipating the next time God asks me to go.

A highlight of each trip has been the boat ride across the Sea of Galilee. I have been fortunate that each trip across has been on a sunny day which has enhanced the beauty of the trip itself. In my experience, this has been a one- way trip as the bus drives around the sea to meet us on the other side. I have now made this voyage four times and, while similar, each has had its differences. Whether more contemplative or joyful, each has been filled with wonder and the realization that Jesus made this same voyage many times, and at least a couple of times without a boat!

On my second trip across the Sea of Galilee, we were not too far into the trip when praise music began playing. Earlier that morning, we had visited the Primacy of Saint Peter where I had so deeply realized that my love for God needed desperately to grow. So in this contemplative and vulnerable state, I began to sing "Shout to the Lord" with my fellow voyagers. This has long been one of my favorite praise and worship songs, although it is true that I would be hard pressed to narrow that list down, as I simply love to praise and worship God in song. The longer I live and the more I experience in life, the more I come to realize the truth of the line "Nothing compares to the promise I have in You."

This day, however, as I was singing the line that precedes that, God spoke one very sacred and confirming word to me. A single word from God can have tremendous power, and this word has given me peace and comfort from the moment it was spoken until now.

Just hours earlier, I had been convicted that my love for God needed to grow, that my love for Him needed to eclipse all else in my life. I had been reminded that He had spoken to me of that years prior and, while ground had been taken and my love for God had grown, He still did not occupy first place in my heart. I was strongly aware that additional growth and change in me needed to occur. In fact, when we reached the middle of the Sea of Galilee, the boat stopped to simply float while Pastor Jerry spoke to us about trust and keeping our focus on Jesus.

Before the boat stopped, however, I was praising God, singing "Shout to the Lord" with a sense of determination and contemplation. I strongly desired to learn to love God more. I wanted there to be no question of where my loyalty lay. I wanted to know that I would not waver and not fall nor forsake my Lord. And as I sang "Forever I'll love you, forever I'll stand," the God of all comfort, who knows the end from the beginning and who knows me better than I know myself, whispered, "Yes."

Chapter 33
Suffer the Children

Growing up, I was not enamored with babies and children. I only babysat a handful of times and was never in demand to be a repeat sitter. Leanne, my sister, was in frequent demand as a sitter, but that is one of the differences between us. In fact, I remember babysitting only three times, none of which went particularly well. The first time I sat for my infant cousin for a couple of hours. I had to change his diaper, something I'd never done before, and I simply could not get the clean one to stay on his little bottom. The second time was for two sisters, one of which asked me why I was fat. The last time was for a brother-sister combination whose parents informed me they didn't believe in disciplining children. You can imagine how well that night went for me. None of these experiences encouraged me to want children of my own; no doubt, they had quite the opposite effect.

My plans for adulthood did not include children at all. I found them to be noisy, unruly, dirty and unpleasant— none of which were attributes I wanted to be part of my future. My plans were to graduate from college and work my way up the corporate ladder, eventually marrying an equally successful man who also had no interest in children, and becoming either the CEO of a large corporation or perhaps the first woman president. Those are not necessarily mutually exclusive goals, but for some reason I never considered achieving both.

I started college but did not graduate the first time through, so I derailed my own dreams of corporate success. Instead, I ultimately married and discovered for the first time a desire to have a child of my own. Initially, pregnancy eluded me. I consulted a gynecologist, and after a number of months he told me that I was not ovulating and would be unable to have children. So I was quite surprised that within two months of receiving that information, I found out I was pregnant! Ultimately, I had three children, Ben and Diona within fifteen months of each other, and Alanna five years later.

How I loved my children! And how much I learned about love from being a mother! Still, while I completely loved and enjoyed my own children, I only endured other children. I allowed sleepovers and visits, and I hosted birthday parties. I was polite and fun and attentive to my children's friends, but the relief I experienced when the moment came that the only children in the house were my own was real.

One summer Sunday, it was announced that volunteers were needed for the Vacation Bible School program. My thought process was this. I have children, therefore I am part of the problem. Since I am part of the problem, I should be part of the solution. And so, with a significant amount of dread, I volunteered. I am fairly certain that had my thought process been known, there would have been some hesitation to accepting my offer to help.

With great wisdom and no doubt prompting from God, I was assigned to assist our Associate Pastor's wife teach the combined fifth and sixth grade class. Amy is a wonderful woman and, in addition to being a pastor's wife at the time, she was also a mother, a trained teacher and my friend. It was a good pairing. Over the two weeks of Vacation Bible School, my heart began to soften just a bit toward children. It was not a big change, but I began to see a little of the impact those two weeks had upon the children.

That fall I began teaching the fifth and sixth grade Sunday School class. Ben had just entered the fifth grade, which put him in my class. The next summer I was the fifth and sixth grade Vacation Bible School teacher, and I continued teaching Sunday School. I moved up with Ben to begin teaching the Junior High Sunday School class and was the Assistant Director for Vacation Bible School, and then the Director for the next two years. I also ended up going on at least one trip with the Junior High and High

School students.

Over those years, God opened both my eyes and my heart to youth ministry. He took a heart that was closed and opened it up and filled it with love. To this day, I still love children. I'm a bit older now, so getting on the floor with little ones is significantly more difficult, but I really have a heart to reach them for Christ while they are young and to show them that they are both important and loved. In fact, several years ago in a Wednesday night prayer meeting, when I requested that we pray for my children, there was a woman who didn't know me well who asked, "How many children do you have?" Before I could respond, my current Associate Pastor's wife exclaimed, "Sondra?! Oh, Sondra has about 16 children!" This is evidence of a heart changed by God.

Chapter 34

Bell's Palsy Promise

During September 1998, I was teaching an Evangelism Explosion class at my church. The class met once weekly, and on the night of September 14 which was also Ben's 15th birthday, I noticed that my left eye was watering excessively. As I looked in the mirror in the ladies' room at church, I thought to myself, "I'm going to wake up with pink eye in the morning." I was not thrilled, but I finished the class and went home for the night.

The next morning, I was pleased to find out that my eye was not matted shut, but quickly became alarmed when I tried to brush my teeth and found I was unable to keep the toothpaste in my mouth. I looked at the mirror and the entire left side of my face was droopy. I thought I had experienced a stroke. My husband rushed me to the emergency room where I was diagnosed with having Bell's Palsy. I was assured that it typically resolved naturally over the course of a few weeks. However, the following January it had not yet resolved, and an MRI was ordered.

After an initial false scare, the MRI did not show anything to be concerned about. I followed doctor's orders regarding keeping my left eye lubricated and covered while I slept, and I continued to wait for it to resolve. I also received prayer for healing a number of times. During one of those prayer sessions, the person praying stated that this is "for a season." I admit that I have since wondered whether the one praying heard that from the Holy Spirit or said it out of knowledge of the typical course of Bell's Palsy. I have also wondered from time to time what defines the length of "a season."

The weeks became months, and the months became a year, then years, then more than a decade, and now more than two decades without complete resolution. There was some minor improvement to the point that my left eye does close completely which is very important for the continued health of that eye, but to this day I have some paralysis and drooping on the left side of my face. I still have occasional but intense pain along my left jaw bone when I sing with exuberance or laugh hard. From time to time, I would continue to ask God to heal it, knowing full well that at this point I am asking for a healing miracle. It is unheard of for Bell's Palsy to resolve after this length of time, and the paralysis is now considered by the medical community to be permanent.

Over the years, God has helped me to become less self- conscious about the appearance of my face. For some time, I would cover the left side of my face with my hand if I were speaking or smiling. I no longer do that. For a number of years, I would only rarely allow my picture to be taken. I no longer refuse but am still fairly self-conscious about it. I was blessed to learn from an inspirational speaker about ten years ago that the smile is more about the eyes than the mouth. This information was very healing for me. Currently, except for my parents, siblings and children, there is no one in my life that has ever seen me without the facial paralysis. Even Wayne has never seen me without it except in pictures. At this point, it has been a fact of my life for so long that I no longer dwell on it, and I no longer look in the mirror and feel as though I am misshapen and grotesque. I don't look at others that way, but I am so much harder on myself.

This past summer I was enjoying a beautiful day when God spoke to me. "If Wayne will pray for you every day, I will heal your Bell's Palsy," He said. I wasn't even thinking about my face. I wasn't asking for healing in that moment. God simply offered me a conditional healing opportunity. By this time, the two sets of 40 days of prayer were complete, and Wayne and I were praying together for the property and for others on a regular basis. The prayers were focused outside our marriage. They were strengthening and changing our marriage, but we were not praying into our marriage. My first feeling was excitement, but it was followed by uncomfortableness. I would have to ask Wayne to pray for me, for my healing, on a daily basis. What if he were to refuse? Or what if he agreed but then didn't follow through? Though I didn't immediately recognize it, these questions were from the enemy. He had no interest in our prayer life growing more intimate. On the other hand, God knew what would happen if I asked Wayne to pray for me.

It took me a couple of weeks to bring the subject up with Wayne. As I should have known, my wonderful, loving and tenderhearted husband immediately agreed to begin praying for me daily. And so from that night, each night before we go to bed, we now lay hands on each other and pray specifically for one another. What a wonderful effect this has had upon our marriage! The love and respect I feel for Wayne continues to grow, and I feel safety that I never imagined I could feel.

After we had been praying together like this for some months, I was scheduled for an in-office medical procedure. It was scheduled to be done before regular office hours in order to accommodate a scheduling conflict my physician had that day. And so, Wayne and I found ourselves walking in with the doctor. As we walked down the hallway, he suddenly asked, "Does the Bell's Palsy still bother you?" I was pretty surprised at the question, as we had never really discussed it before although he had been my physician for about a decade. I described the intermittent pain I still experienced as well as the residual self-consciousness. He mentioned that he had read an article earlier that week that discussed the possibility of a treatment for resolution of long-term Bell's Palsy paralysis!

As he prepped me for the scheduled procedure, I told him about the promise from God and the commitment to prayer Wayne and I had made. I stated that I did not know whether this article he read would have anything to do with the promised healing, but that I did consider his bringing it up as confirmation that I had heard correctly from God.

At this point, he asked, "You prayer for each other every day?"

"Yes," I responded. "Out loud?" he asked.

"Yes, out loud," I confirmed.

He then told me that he had recently read another article—like me, he is an avid reader—that had stated, based upon a study, that couples who prayed out loud together routinely had a zero percent divorce rate. We discussed some other topics throughout the remainder of the procedure, including how the writing of this book was going, and when the procedure was complete, Wayne drove me home to rest.

When I returned for my follow-up appointment, my doctor let me know he had done additional research and wanted to know if I wanted to find out if I was a candidate for the treatment. I decided to do so. As a result, early the next January, I received the treatment. My doctor was so excited during the procedure. If I understood him correctly, this was the first attempt at this in the United States and he had only found one article about it at all. The last thing he said before we left that day is, "Keep praying."

At the time I initially wrote this chapter it had been 18 days since the treatment, and I was waiting to see if it worked. If there were to be positive results, I was told they could take months to occur. I didn't know then whether the treatment worked or not. I didn't know whether this was the method God had chosen to heal my face.

Today, as I update this chapter, I can add that there was some improvement and I no longer have the intense pain when singing or laughing. God may have directed my physician to this obscure article in order that I would receive this treatment in order to address the pain and He may choose to heal me by another innovative medical treatment or by a divine miracle. I don't know. What I do know is this. Two-plus decades of paralysis is by no means insurmountable for God. God told me that if my husband would pray for me daily, He would heal my Bell's Palsy. God's promises are always true. So, if my husband prays for me daily—and he has, and I have every reason to believe he will continue—then God will heal the remainder of the paralysis in my face.

Chapter 35

Peace in the Battle

In the first year of our marriage, I received word that Wayne had been accused of a heinous crime. We had met and married quickly; and subsequently, I did not know him nearly as well as I would have known him had we dated for years prior to marrying. In fact, we were both accused of being involved in the crime, but the initial word I received only mentioned Wayne. Wayne assured me of his innocence. Still, the accuser was someone I had known for more than a decade, and the accused was someone I had known for less than two years.

I needed wisdom desperately. Wayne and I were supposed to be headed to a small group meeting that night, but neither of us was in the emotional state to be in a group, even a small one. We contacted our associate pastor and made arrangements for him to pray with us for wisdom. The small group was meeting in his home, and he took us quickly and quietly into another room when we arrived.

The drive from our home to our associate pastor's home was an hour in length and, at the outset, I wasn't sure I even wanted to be in the car with Wayne. So, as he drove us, I cried out to God asking for wisdom to know whether my husband was innocent or guilty of the accusation. I was distraught, and I have found that being in an extreme emotional state can make it difficult to hear the typically still, small voice of God. After some minutes of prayer, I asked God for a sign—I would reach out to hold Wayne's hand and I asked God to cause me to feel repulsed if he were guilty. It was a truly horrible accusation, and I was already feeling only negative emotions—fear, repulsion, anger, grief—feeling something that I was actually already feeling was not really a big ask in this case. With trepidation, I reached for Wayne's hand and, as he closed his fingers over mine, I was enveloped from head to toe with a sense of relief. This was not at all what I expected! I asked God to confirm, and I sensed His presence.

So, while we entered our associate pastor's home, not knowing what to expect in the immediate future and still feeling fear, anger, grief and repulsion, I, at least, entered his home confident that the accusation was completely false and my husband was innocent of the crime. We sat alone until the pastor got the group under way, and then we were prayed for and prayed over. We then made the long drive home, shock at the circumstances we found ourselves in rendering both of us quiet.

Within a few days, I found myself driving alone to

the courthouse in Shelby County. As I drove, fear began welling up in a powerful way, so I cried out to God for help. As I was praying, God gave me a song! It was short, sweet and personal; a song written by God just for me! The words to the song are:

"'Let My peace fill your heart,' says the Lord.

"'Let My peace fill your heart,' says the Lord.

"Peace that passes all understanding—

"'Let My peace fill your heart,' says the Lord."

I found His peace filled my heart as I sang the song He had given me. To this day, I can sing this song and be filled with peace no matter the circumstances I find myself in. Once I was peaceful, God gave me another song, one that was published and that I knew from times of praise and worship: "Shouts of Joy" by Paul Wilbur. This is a song of victory. And so, on the 15-minute drive to the courthouse that day, God spoke both peace and victory into my soul. He knew what was coming next.

At the courthouse, I found out that the accusation was against me as well. How thankful I am that God prepared me with a message of peace and victory! Otherwise, that news could have been so much more damaging. Hearing that I was also accused had the effect of solidifying my knowledge of Wayne's innocence, because I certainly knew of my own.

It was not long before this turned into a battle on another front. The false accusation led to a renewed custody battle, which was temporarily lost. Before this was over, it escalated to the point that Wayne and I required the services of three attorneys and a private detective. It caused great strain on our children, our families and our finances. It could have destroyed our marriage, but we had turned to God and He had other plans.

Eventually—and it was a long haul—the accuser recanted and the ordeal was essentially over. To this day there are residual effects that we deal with in family relationships and finances. However, God did not allow our marriage to fall apart, even though that appears to be what the enemy planned. Instead, we grew closer to each other and to Him. God used what the enemy meant for evil to mold and fashion us to be more like His image, more secure in each other and in Him. God has worked miracles of love and forgiveness in our hearts toward those who wronged us in the process and continues to help us to rebuild financially. We were never alone, never abandoned, but were always in the presence of the God who granted us peace and promised us victory.

Chapter 36
Vacation Assignments

Wayne and I try to allow God to arrange our lives, rather than self-arranging. Certainly we don't always get it right, but it is so glorious when we do hear correctly from God and obey Him. We were invited to spend this a recent Christmas with Ben and Edward in Florida. Getting away to a warm state from an Indiana winter for a week sounded wonderful! And, spending that time with my children during my favorite holiday sounded even more wonderful. The question remained whether it was God's will for Wayne and me. Wayne and I began praying about it and felt that it was indeed God's will that we go to Florida.

I sometimes marvel that many envision God as someone who is always saying "No!" and "Don't!" wanting to prevent all fun and joy until I remember that before I truly knew Him, I had a similar impression. The truth is that obedience to Him is a grand adventure, and He delights in us. He does say both "No" and Don't," but that is to either protect us from harm or to get us to His greater plan for our lives rather than allowing us to settle for our own lesser plan.

Still, once we heard we were to go to Florida for Christmas, the question remained how we were to get there. I looked at flights since one never knows what winter will do to northern roads, but didn't feel that was what we were supposed to do. So, drive it was. Next thing we needed to know was the timing and the route. Ultimately, we felt we were to drive to South Carolina on the Saturday before Christmas and attend the Saturday night service at a sister church where there were many people we know and love. Then, we were to continue on to Atlanta and attend church with a beautiful pastor we had only recently met who was planting a new church in that area. We would then continue on to Florida following the service.

A couple of days before we were to leave, we heard that the South Carolina church was not actually going to have a service that night, but a "come and go" communion service instead. I asked Wayne whether we were still to go there or go straight to Atlanta to save some travel time and arrive more rested. Wayne waited for a leading and then told me we were still to go to South Carolina first. And so, we left Saturday morning according to plan.

As we drove through the mountains of Tennessee, we received a phone call from the pastor in Atlanta.

"Would you be willing to share for a few minutes about what Christmas means to you in the service tomorrow?" he asked. I stated that I would be happy to do so. He went on to explain that it only needed to be about five minutes, but that I could have more time if I needed it. He also stated that it was possible there would be a number of people who had no idea of the meaning of Christmas. After we hung up, I realized that, perhaps because of the difficulties of cell phone usage in the mountains, I was unclear whether I had committed myself to speaking or both of us. Speaking in public doesn't frighten me, but that is not true of Wayne. Regardless of whether it was one or both of us, we desired only to say what God would have us to say, and so we prayed for wisdom and direction in the car. Then I texted five prayer warriors to pray on our behalf. As we continued travelling, I listened for the still, small voice to lead me.

We arrived in South Carolina without incident and went in to receive communion. It was truly a moment of intimacy with our Lord as the pastor, whom we love dearly, administered communion to us after sharing with us personally. We were able to greet a number of beloved friends as they came in to receive communion and were waiting for two other couples to arrive who had made arrangements to go out to dinner with us that night before we continued our journey.

Before we left for dinner, the pastor's wife came in. She came over to me and we began speaking with one another. She had received some very difficult news just a few hours earlier, and the Holy Spirit helped me to hold and comfort her. As we were leaving the sanctuary, the Holy Spirit let me know that those few minutes were the reason we were to go through South Carolina that night. How great is God's love for us that He would send love and a hug from Indiana to South Carolina at just the right moment! I felt both extremely blessed and humbled to have been used of Him in such a way.

Dinner with such dear friends was a wonderful interlude before driving the last couple of hours to Atlanta that night. As the meal ended, we also prayed together that God would give us the words He wanted spoken the next morning. And, by the time we arrived at our hotel in Atlanta, I knew the message I was to convey. I thought of making an outline or jotting down some bullet points, but was assured that the Holy Spirit would give me the words to speak and that I was simply to trust Him and speak from my heart what I heard Him say.

The next morning, Wayne and I left early to find the building the church was meeting in, desiring both to have extra time if needed for navigation and to have a few minutes with the pastor and his wife before service, if possible. Needing only to backtrack one block, we arrived about a half hour before start of service. After greetings and hugs were exchanged, I let the pastor know that God had given me a word for the service, but that it would require more than five minutes. He assured me that I would have as much time as was needed.

As people arrived for the service, I watched, smiling at this tender beginning of something new. We were introduced to many of the attendees as they entered and, as I looked over the congregation from my seat, God gave me another word for them. I was to give both. The service started with praise and worship in four different languages. I did my best to sing in all four, not knowing even what language I was praising in, except for the song in English. The pastor's wife, who was praising next to me, told me a week later when we stopped in Atlanta on our return trip that I was a natural in Swahili! After the praise, the pastor was announcing what the order of service would be and, in doing so, stated, "Miss Sondra will be last. I know that God has given her the word for us today."

There was a scripture reading from the second chapter of Luke, two speakers and a special musical number that would precede me. At this point, Wayne relaxed, realizing that he was not expected by the pastor or by God to speak in the service that morning. We listened to all that was offered in the service, and then it was my turn to speak. As I took the microphone and turned to face the congregation, I could feel the Holy Spirit upon me in power in a manner I don't believe I had ever felt before.

He helped me to deliver both words for this

congregation. The one I received that morning to be delivered first was a word of encouragement and exhortation for the congregation—they were not to despise the time of small beginnings, but to recognize that little is much when God is in it. The Holy Spirit prompted me to speak of the loaves and fishes and admonish them that Jesus had to both bless and break the loaves and fishes for them to be multiplied. They needed to embrace the time of breaking, knowing that it was necessary for growth.

The second word, which I had received the night before, was about Jesus, Lord and Savior. God had reminded me of two precious Christmas memories— Christmas Eve birthday parties for Jesus with my parents and siblings and my grandmother singing "The Old Rugged Cross" during the Christmas season. The message was that Jesus entered the world as an infant so as to be completely approachable. Yet, his birth was always intended to lead to the cross and resurrection. We must not only celebrate the baby, but also embrace the man. Between Jesus' birth and his redemptive work on the cross, He suffered every way that we suffer. He knows what it is to be lied about. He knows what it is to be spat upon. He knows what it is to be hungry. He knows what it is to be betrayed. So, the man is no less approachable than the infant because He truly knows the human experience. Yes, we can and should celebrate the baby, but we need to behold and embrace the man! The Holy Spirit gave me the words to speak, the intensity, the inflections and the timing! He is trustworthy to do as He says He will do.

What a fantastic way to begin our vacation! Wayne and I sought God about leisure time with our children and, when we chose to seek Him first and then be obedient, He added on to us thrills and adventure in the Kingdom of God.

Chapter 37
Rainbow of Assurance

Alanna had graduated from high school. The graduation ceremony was over. Her salutatorian speech was a thing of the past. The parties and celebrations had been fun but were done. And, the summer had flown by. The day I both looked forward to and dreaded in equal measure had arrived. I had to take my baby girl to an apartment in West Lafayette so that she could begin working toward her bachelor's degree at Purdue University. I would be leaving her to live with two complete strangers and trusting that she would attend classes, study hard, be responsible, make wise choices, remain safe and not lose her faith for the next four years. I was well aware that those were all things I had pretty much failed at the first time I attended college.

On the other hand, Alanna was leaving home for college as a more mature young woman and was certainly more grounded in her faith than her mother had been. Still, she was the last of my children to leave home and the first to go to college. My excitement for her future, my pride in her accomplishments, and my fear that she would experience hurt were all extremely high. In this state, we packed the car with her belongings, prayed for safety and headed to West Lafayette.

No doubt Alanna had some fears of her own, but they were well hidden by her high level of excitement as we made the drive. I was determined that she would only know of my excitement and pride and worked hard to keep my own fear suppressed. However, I could find no way to hide just how much I was going to miss having her at home. Throughout the day, I prayed for her safety and for help with being supportive but not overbearing.

We arrived at the apartment complex without incident, and having signed the lease earlier in the summer, we simply had to pick up the keys and begin carrying boxes into her room. We met one of her new apartment mates who explained some basic rules they had developed to prevent tension and misunderstanding, all of which seemed reasonable. She helped us carry Alanna's belongings in and left us to get her settled.

From there we headed to the Wal-Mart that was nearly adjacent to the apartment complex where we shopped for basics. I wanted to know that she had sufficient food and toilet paper to get through the first few weeks while she was acclimating to being on her own. Wayne and I assisted with arranging her things, hanging the shower curtain and making certain the habitat for

Dieter and Baby, Alanna's ferrets, was reassembled. Finally, there wasn't much more I could do to delay the inevitable leave-taking, so I suggested we go out to eat before we left for home.

My brother and sister had both attended Purdue, and it had become a tradition that our mother would take them out to eat at the Hour Time restaurant when she visited. I had also been there with her on at least one occasion when we visited Leanne and Vince at Purdue. Naturally, that's where I suggested we go, thinking to continue the tradition.

We ordered our meals, and they were served and were delicious; however, we had only eaten a very small portion of our respective meals when a severe storm began. The winds were high enough, and there was apparently potential for a tornado, that the restaurant staff evacuated all the diners and staff to an inner hallway of the adjacent Best Western hotel to shelter in place. I don't remember how long we were in that hallway with our fellow diners, but I remember it seemed to be a significant amount of time.

When the staff allowed us to return to our table, our food had turned cold and, instead of asking for it to be reheated, we decided to forego eating the remainder and order dessert instead. Desserts fully enjoyed, it was time to return Alanna to her apartment and drive home without her. I was somber on the short drive from the restaurant to the apartment complex. As I recall, we were all somewhat quiet.

We arrived at the complex all too quickly and, storm over, got out of the car for a goodbye hug. As Alanna and I hugged goodbye, I was praying and struggling not to cry. Her back was to three apartment buildings, the middle of which contained her home for the next year. As I released her from the hug, I looked up and was amazed at what I saw. Directly above her apartment building and spanning from the inside wall of each adjacent building was a beautiful bright and distinct rainbow! In that moment, God used the sign of His promise never to destroy the earth by water again to let me know without a doubt that He would be taking care of Alanna. In that moment, I felt such joy and peace, knowing that His hands were an infinitely better place for Alanna to be than mine. Immediately, I had Alanna and Wayne look to see what I was seeing. What comfort God gave to all of us in that moment!

We exchanged additional goodbye hugs, this time with joy, thanksgiving and praise! I was able to watch Alanna walk to her apartment with peace in my heart, and Wayne and I drove home, comforted by the One Who loves us best.

Chapter 38

A Gift of Life

Not quite a decade ago, my father's kidneys began to fail. Unfortunately, the failure progressed fairly rapidly. It was my habit to get up each morning and start my day with a time of prayer on my knees. Each morning for about a year, I prayed that my father's kidneys would be healed. However, they continued to deteriorate. Diona's wedding was approaching. From the time Diona was a little girl, she had dreamed of her grandfather walking her down the aisle at her wedding. That was the plan, but Dad was deteriorating rapidly and, while we did not warn Diona, several of us were concerned about his ability to do so.

All three of his children and each of their spouses offered to give Dad a kidney. He refused outright to consider receiving that gift from any of us. The day of the wedding arrived and Dad, quite possibly through the sheer determination to bring joy to his beloved granddaughter, escorted our beautiful bride down the aisle. Almost immediately following the wedding day, it was necessary for Dad to begin dialysis therapy. As he continued to refuse to consider receiving a kidney from one of his children, I continued to pray for his kidneys to be healed each morning and added the request that he would tolerate dialysis in the interim and that it would be as comfortable for him as possible.

What I did not request was a kidney for my father from another source. While I wanted my father's healing, I felt, right or wrong, that asking for him to receive a kidney was also asking for the death of someone else's loved one. I simply could not bring myself to do so. And so morning after morning, I faithfully got on my knees and asked God to heal my father's kidneys. Not once did I request that a transplant be made available to him.

At the very end of the year, Alanna and I were on vacation in Florida where we had accompanied Diona and her husband for a delayed honeymoon. The honeymooners had their own suite, and Alanna and I were enjoying the Florida warmth. Each morning, I continued to rise before the others and get on my knees to pray. Each prayer included a plea that my father's kidneys be healed. But, this morning was different. As I prayed and very much to my surprise, I heard myself say, "Please get a kidney for Dad." My first instinct was to "take it back." I felt panicked and actually started to say, "God, I didn't mean that," when the Holy Spirit stopped me. I paused and found assurance flowing over me that the prayer had been of the Holy Spirit. I finished praying, prepared for the day and went with Alanna to enjoy some pool time in the sun.

Some hours later, we returned to our suite where we had left our cellphones. My cellphone had an urgent request on it to call my mother. When I called, I was told that Dad might be getting a kidney! In fact, the following day, New Year's Day, my father received the gift of a healthy kidney and a new lease on life! Mom and Dad both insisted that we remain in Florida so as to not interrupt the honeymoon. And so, it was a number of days later before we returned home to Indiana and to my parents.

I was elated for my father and what that meant to our family. I was simultaneously dejected for the family who had lost a loved one and began praying for them in addition to praying that the transplant would be successful. After some weeks had passed, God arranged for me to learn additional details. I found out that at the time of my prayer, the young man whose kidney was ultimately successfully transplanted into my father had already passed into eternity. At the time of my prayer, donor decisions were not yet made. You see, not only did God help me to pray the right prayer for my dad at the exact moment of need, allowing me to be a part of the miracle, but He also honored my heart. I asked for the kidney only after this precious family had already lost their loved one. How great and loving is our God!

As a result of the transplant, Dad lived for an

additional eight years. Many of those years are no doubt years that he would not have had to spend on this earth with his family had he not received that precious gift. All those years, he was free from the need for three times weekly dialysis sessions which was a great improvement in quality of life. I am thankful for the bonus years we were given, and I'm thankful to know that we will ultimately spend eternity together with our Lord.

Chapter 39

Limitless Prayer

I love to pray. It is one of the most exhilarating and most humbling activities in life. It is so incredible to consider that the God who created and sustains the universe listens to what I have to say. It is humbling to consider that He takes the time to direct the path my prayers take, always when I am listening, and sometimes to my great surprise. It is amazing that He chooses to work through my prayers. And, it is nearly unfathomable that He will help me to pray about what is being discussed in the throne room of heaven at any given moment. I don't know why God has chosen to work through the prayers of His children, but I do know that praying what is on the heart of God is powerful beyond what I can imagine.

I love to pray. I crave the intimacy I feel with my Creator when I feel His presence through prayer. I delight in the words of comfort, wisdom, revelation, and correction I receive as we talk. I love to pray, and yet I still find it difficult at times to sustain the prayer life I desire. Earlier this week, I asked God how this can be. Why is it difficult to do something I enjoy so much? I feel the answer I received is that the battle against prayer waged by the enemy is so intense that it discourages us from praying even though it is so desirable.

It makes sense that the enemy would not want us to engage in prayer. It is a time of intimacy with our Heavenly Father. It is a time where God can speak to us as we tune out the world around us. He has spoken so much to me through my prayers on behalf of others. One time when I was serving on a ministry team that made itself available for prayer at the end of service, a young woman whom I had never met approached me. She was pregnant, unmarried and afraid. She had not yet told her parents, and she was feeling guilt and shame. As I prayed with and for this young woman, I found myself praying, at the inspiration of the Holy Spirit, that her situation had not taken God by surprise. I have to trust that this young woman received help from the prayer as I don't believe I ever saw her again, but I know that I received tremendous help from that prayer! While I had long been taught that God knows the end from the beginning and that Christ paid for all sin—past, present and future—that was the moment it became real to me.

One of the great highlights of my week was Saturday morning Women's Prayer. The group of ladies I met with each week for several years are wonderful prayer warriors. Because of that and because of teaching and admonition we have received, the hour or so that we met together was dedicated to finding and praying the petition that was on God's heart. We prayed listening for the prompting of the Holy Spirit to get us to what was being discussed in the throne room.

What may be the single greatest revelation I have ever received about prayer, I received in one of these meetings. As I was praying, the Holy Spirit told me to claim for Jesus Christ the property and building belonging to an entirely different religion. He told me to pray for the souls of all who worship there to come to Him. I heard it clearly, but it was a seemingly impossible thing to claim. I hesitated and, in my mind, I said to the Holy Spirit, "That's a big ask." Instantly He responded, "You can't pray too big. You can only pray too small." In that moment, I chose to believe what the Holy Spirit said. I prayed that prayer and I made that claim. And, as He brings it back to me, I continue to do so, believing that one day it will be accomplished.

What power is in those two sentences! God is limitless in and of Himself, but we limit Him, we box Him in, by praying too small. At His prompting, we should feel confident in praying the big prayers. Two short sentences of instruction uttered by the Holy Spirit to my heart one Saturday morning revolutionized my prayer life. I want to be certain that I do not ever limit what God wants to do but continue to ask the "big ask" as He reveals His heart to me.

Chapter 40

Indescribable Intimacy

I t was the second Sunday our group was in Israel on my third trip to the Holy Land. We were in Galilee and had arranged to have a church service on the balcony on the top floor of the Jesus Boat Museum. The balcony itself is unremarkable, gray concrete in a semicircle, but the view over the Sea of Galilee is spectacular. Wayne and I were among the first to arrive on the balcony, so I looked out at the beautiful, calm sea and thought of Jesus and the many times He crossed it, some of them even in a boat!

Once everyone had arrived, I found a place to stand and continued contemplating how much I loved this land that my Savior had walked. There were a few opening remarks regarding the area we were in and feeling free to move around during the service; then Pastor Taylor and Molly, the son and daughter of our senior pastor, moved to the front to begin leading worship.

It has long been my habit to close my eyes during praise and worship when I am in a group setting, opening them only to glance briefly at the words of the song if I do not know it by heart. I do this for a number of reasons. It helps me to keep my focus on God rather than being distracted by those around me. I am less likely to be concerned with distracting others or what I look like when my eyes are closed. I feel greater freedom to worship, and I have found I am more likely to experience and recognize the presence of God this way.

As the first song began, I closed my eyes to enter into worship of my Lord. Before even the first phrase had been completely sung, I heard Jesus whisper to me, "I want to look into your eyes." I have had many wonderful, even miraculous experiences in Israel, but this was well beyond anything I expected or even dared to dream. And so, I opened my eyes. Not wanting to chance being distracted by anything whatsoever, I looked toward the concrete wall over the head of the worship leaders. Immediately I could feel Jesus looking into my eyes. I could not see His face, but I could feel His gaze in a way that I am unlikely to be able to convey fully. He was looking into my eyes and much deeper into my very being.

Jesus continued to look into my eyes throughout the entire song. The emotions I felt were staggering in their intensity. I felt deeply loved as though every cell in my body was loved individually and as a whole. I felt beautiful to my very core. It was all I could do to keep my eyes open, the intensity was overwhelming. I willed my eyes to stay open, not wanting to miss a blink of this experience with Jesus.

A way to approximate the intensity is to think on the most decadently rich dessert you can imagine, so rich that only a few bites are necessary to take care of your sweet tooth. As you take each bite, your mouth simultaneously experiences overwhelming pleasure and a sense that another bite will be more pleasure than you can withstand. You want more, and yet each bite feels as though it is all you can handle. This experience was like that, but even more intense.

A number of things were happening to me as the song continued as a distant backdrop to Jesus focusing on me. I could feel Jesus' desire to be with me. I am His bride, and I could tell that He longed to spend time with me, and that He was looking forward to the day when I will spend all eternity with Him and be able to speak with Him face to face. Because of this, I felt both cherished and beautiful. I had never in my life felt truly beautiful and, since having Bell's Palsy and the resulting years of a face with muscles that were not fully functioning, I had felt truly abhorrent in appearance for nearly two decades. Jesus changed that for me in those moments. I am looking forward to the day when my face is fully healed, but I no longer feel ugly. God finds me beautiful now, and I choose to believe Him.

Another change that was occurring in me was an

increase in my sense of self-worth. Jesus sought me out personally and intimately. I am valuable to Him. It also increased my still-limited understanding of how greatly I am loved. The love that I could feel coming from His eyes is indescribable. There was no censure, no "if onlys," no "excepts," no "buts;" just complete and unconditional love.

I suspect that even more was accomplished in those minutes than I know now. Some six years later, I find I have a greater desire than ever to reflect Jesus accurately to the world around me. My longing for the day when I enter eternity has grown immeasurably. I have a greater love for those around me. No doubt there is much more that will be revealed as the days and years ahead unfold.

At the end of the first song, I felt my nervous system had reached the saturation point and that I must close my eyes or risk melting away into the concrete. However, as my eyes closed, I heard, "I'm not done yet." I reopened my eyes to find Jesus still gazing deeply into them, which He continued to do through the first verse of the second worship song.

I cannot feel that I have described this conversation with God in a way that does it full justice. Nonetheless, to say that I long to see my Lord face to face, that my love for Him has grown exponentially, and that I have been changed forever by those few moments on a concrete balcony overlooking the Sea of Galilee would be both completely accurate and entirely understated.

What a tender, loving Savior we have!

Afterword

I am truly an ordinary woman who has been extraordinarily fortunate to have recognized the voice of God at a number of times in her life. As much as God loves me, He also loves you. As often as He speaks with me, He wants to speak with you and with both of us even more often than this book has described. He loves us, cherishes us, and wants to have a dynamic relationship with us.

I have described a number of ways that He has spoken to me, but as He has created each of us uniquely, your own experience will also be unique. A great mistake that many, including me, have made is to compare ourselves to others. So, it is my hope and prayer that you will not find yourself discouraged if you have not had the same experiences I have had, but rather you will find yourself encouraged that God does speak and that you will seek to recognize His voice among the many others that vie for your attention.

May God bless you with a hunger for Him that only He can fill.

About the Author

Sondra Haggard is a practicing pharmacist, licensed in Indiana, Kentucky, and Michigan. She has three children, Ben, Diona, and Alanna, who brought two sons-in-love into her life, Edward and Will. During her lifetime, she has lived in Indiana, Taiwan, and England and currently lives in Indiana, with her husband, Wayne. She is placed by God in Plainfield Christ Fellowship and has been under the ministry of Pastor Jerry Keller for more than two decades.

You may connect with Sondra in the following ways:

Email
Sondrascribe@gmail.com

Postal Mail
230 South Perry Road #1110
Plainfield, IN 46168

www.ingramcontent.com/pod-product-compliance
Lightning Source LLC
Chambersburg PA
CBHW051514120626

46551CB00012B/920